SAND, GRIT
AND
DANGEROUS
SUPPLY MISSIONS

THE UNSUNG CIVILIAN
HEROES OF THE IRAQ WAR

WRITTEN BY KEITH RICHARD

Inspired Forever Books
Dallas, Texas

Sand, Grit and Dangerous Supply Missions
The Unsung Civilian Heroes of the Iraq War
Copyright © 2025 Keith Richard

All rights reserved, including the right of reproduction in whole or in part in any form without prior written permission, except in the case of brief quotations embodied in critical reviews and certain other noncommercial uses permitted by copyright law.

Inspired Forever Books
Dallas, Texas
(888) 403-2727
https://inspiredforeverbooks.com
"Words With Lasting Impact™"

Paperback ISBN: 978-1-948903-88-2
Library of Congress Number: 2025907843
Printed in the United States of America

Disclaimer: This book is based on real events and personal experiences. Certain names, locations, and identifying details have been changed to protect the privacy of individuals involved. The author has made every effort to ensure the accuracy of the information presented, but readers should be aware that memories and perceptions can vary. The views expressed are solely those of the author and do not necessarily reflect those of the publisher. The publisher assumes no responsibility for errors or omissions in the content of this book. All information is provided 'as is' with no guarantees of completeness, accuracy, or timeliness. The reader assumes full responsibility for any actions taken based on the information provided in this book. This content is intended for informative and educative purposes only.

TABLE OF CONTENTS

1. The Decision..1
2. Orientation..11
3. Arrival and Introductions...21
4. Overview, Confusion and Disorder............................33
5. A Hot Seat and Some Cold Realities..........................43
6. The Anaconda Corkscrew..57
7. Iraq: Hearts, Minds and IED's....................................67
8. Chaos, Frustration and a Target on our Back............77
9. All Hell Breaks Loose..87
10. Aftermath..99
11. Home on the Shooting Range..................................109
12. The Fallout and Wounds You Can't See.................121
13. Return Home and Litigation...................................133
14. Conclusion..143

CHAPTER 1
THE DECISION

As I reflect on my personal and professional life, I realize I wouldn't be the person I am today without my wonderful, strong, and understanding wife, Lana.

Our story begins in June 1981 when we first met. Having both grown up in small towns along the Gulf Coast of Mississippi, we attended high schools that were only about a mile apart. Students from one school rarely associated with those from the other, but we were all proud Mississippians. Once we graduated, old rivalries faded, and many of us found ourselves in the same circles, sharing the same friends.

I had just completed my freshman year at Ole Miss, the University of Mississippi, located a few hours north in Oxford. Lana was about to enter the 11th grade. One of the highlights of the summer was the Biloxi Fishing Rodeo, where I was introduced to Lana by one of her closest friends. I still remember the moment I met my future wife. We were introduced by a friend of Lana's whom I knew through a high school acquaintance. Her friend said, "Keith, this is Lana, and she needs a ride home tonight. Can you take her?" We looked at each other, and of course, I said,

"Absolutely." We chatted for a bit, and I drove her home. So, while Lana and I would see each other at various events along the Mississippi coast and hang out occasionally, I was always thinking about heading back to school.

As I transitioned into my sophomore year at Ole Miss, we stayed in touch and would sometimes reconnect when I returned home. At the end of that year, I was out water skiing with some friends, enjoying a few cold beers, when we decided to take the boat to the Ocean Springs Fishing Rodeo on the beach. As we walked under the large tent, I spotted Lana. I turned to my friends and said, "I'm going to ask Lana on a date." I walked over, asked her what she was doing that night, and we made plans to meet at a local disco in Biloxi. That evening changed everything. As the saying goes, "Life has never been the same." Here we are, nearly 41 years later, with two adult sons and five grandchildren.

My own story begins with my Depression-era parents. I was the youngest of their four boys. My mother, whose maiden name was Flanagan, came from a predominantly Irish background and was the youngest of twelve children. My father had a diverse ethnic heritage, with a strong Cajun French influence. Both worked blue-collar jobs—Dad as an auto parts salesman and Mom as an insurance office assistant. We grew up in a lower-middle-class family but never truly wanted for anything.

Our life together truly took shape when Lana and I had our first son, Keith Jr., in March of 1984. Lana was a dependent of a proud military veteran who had served in World War II, Korea, and Vietnam, we decided it was important for me to finish my degree while she stayed at home with her parents. Keith Jr. was born at Keesler AFB in Biloxi. Lana is the youngest of four girls and I am the youngest of four boys. The siblings are the same years apart. Oh, Lana and I share the same birthday. We have several strange and unique commonalities in our life and families. Maybe our life together was meant to be.

Chapter 1 The Decision

After graduating, I traveled to Houston, Texas, to look for employment, staying with my oldest brother, Leo Jr. Within a few weeks, I landed a job with a trucking company owned by Montgomery Ward, a well-known retailer that, unfortunately, would not survive the emerging "big box" era. For me, though, it was a promising career start.

After four years with Montgomery Ward, I found myself dissatisfied with my position and our personal situation. We had been transferred to Kansas City and then to Denver. Experiencing a few blizzards and several feet of snow in Denver convinced us it was time to move closer to home.

In 1988, job hunting was nothing like it is today. Without the internet or email, the main way to find a job was through newspaper ads. As the youngest of four, I was still "Momma's boy," and she would frequently send me cut-out job listings from newspapers along with long, handwritten letters. One of these opportunities was with Sea-Land Services in New Orleans as a Maintenance Supervisor. After a couple of interviews, I was offered the job, and we moved to Slidell, Louisiana—not quite home, but close enough.

This is where my real professional growth began. At Montgomery Ward, I had moved beyond book learning and had to navigate the complexities of customers and managing a unionized workforce. At Sea-Land, I took things up a notch and solidified my commitment to transportation and logistics.

During my 11 years with the company, I gained invaluable experience in leadership roles. By 1994, I was recruited to a position in Dallas as the Corridor Manager for the Southeast Region, then for the Western Region, and eventually as the Director of the Western Network. Lana still swears that the only reason I took the job was to move to the home of the Dallas Cowboys. She's not entirely wrong—I am a lifelong Cowboys fan, though the last 20 years have been rough. At the height of my passion, no one could watch a game with me.

The kid from Mississippi was making good, managing a $120 million logistics operation with a team of 60 professionals. We oversaw equipment control, intermodal and trucking activity, procurement, carrier contracts, and Freight Bill Audit and Payment (FBAP), a process ensuring shippers only paid for actual shipment costs and not carrier errors.

During this intense period, Lana held down the fort, raising our boys and keeping things running smoothly. Our youngest, Aaron, was born during this time. She may have even started to consider herself a Texan—and possibly, a Cowboys fan.

Then, in 1999, Sea-Land was acquired by Maersk, the global shipping giant. With such a drastic shift in ownership and culture, things changed. I took my accomplishments and experience to Ryder Logistics as a Director, only to be quickly recruited again, this time as a Vice President with an intermodal trucking company leading the Gulf region. We expanded operations and revenue by over 300% in two years and improved profitability by nearly 30%. It seemed like my upward career trajectory was continuing.

However, as often happens, things hit a snag, and I found myself unemployed for the first time in my career. While I had a comfortable severance package, I never saw it as a vacation. I felt a sense of urgency to grab a rung on the ladder and find my next opportunity, not just for me but for my family.

Lana, ever the strong and opinionated, the voice of reason, told me something that struck a chord: "Keith, you're like a dog chasing its tail. You don't know what you're chasing, you'll never catch it, and if you did, you wouldn't know what to do with it." She was right. I needed focus.

Lana frequently made these kinds of comments, recognizing that I was searching for something without a clear vision for my future. This was her way of encouraging me to slow down, stop, and focus on my goals.

Chapter 1 The Decision

Well, that's Lana. Her friends and family love her for her candor, passion, and, most importantly, absolute loyalty. In this case, she had hit the nail on the head.

My beautiful wife doesn't hold back and tends to say what is on her mind. I have made the mistake on some occasions of using the term "Lana's way or the highway," and it typically doesn't turn out well.

At home, the boys and I knew that Lana *ruled the roost*—and we gladly followed her lead. She's loving and deeply caring, but also a firm believer in order and absolute respect. Sure, we had our moments (what family doesn't?), but often… she was right.

In the end, we always knew just how lucky we were. Lana is an incredible wife and mother—our steady compass, our heart, and the glue that holds us together.

One of the greatest examples of Lana's powerful personality came when our oldest son, Keith Jr., was in the 11th grade. At the time, Keith was a defensive tackle for his high school team—which, as you can imagine, meant he was (and still is) a pretty big guy.

But size didn't matter when Lana stepped in. Her presence, determination, and authority were more than enough to command respect—and Keith Jr. knew better than to test her resolve. Let's just say, even the toughest defensive tackle didn't stand a chance against Mom's willpower!

One Sunday morning, as we were getting ready for church, Lana was in full command—getting everyone organized, aligned, and out the door. Keith Jr. and I didn't waste any time; we grabbed our things, rounded up our youngest (Aaron, who's not exactly a small guy), and piled into the truck. Meanwhile, Lana was still inside, making sure everything else was in order. In that moment, the three of us looked at each other and silently agreed: *we really need to stop questioning her and just follow instructions the first time.* Lesson learned—again!

As for my job search, I still didn't quite know what I was looking for, but with Lana's encouragement, I figured I'd recognize it when I saw it. So, I started applying for various leadership positions in the transportation industry, including with prior employers.

Then, I came across a job posting for a senior transportation position overseas with Halliburton and KBR. It was vague but intriguing. I applied, got an interview, and quickly learned the job wasn't in Dubai as I had assumed—it was in Kuwait, supporting military supply chain operations in the Middle East. The recruiter was uncertain about the exact location, but his job was to find candidates, not be an expert in the company's business, so I didn't dwell on it.

However, Lana was immediately concerned and hesitant about the opportunity due to the location. I explained that we should at least consider it, especially given the compensation. Growing up on the Mississippi coast, we knew people who worked offshore and overseas in the oil and gas industry, making the idea somewhat more familiar.

Soon after, a KBR representative scheduled an interview in Houston. I found the speed of the process interesting. Higher level positions typically do not go this quickly. Apparently, this position was being expedited.

The interview in Houston was scheduled shortly thereafter. Lana and I drove to Houston together and spent a couple days enjoying the area. When I finally walked into the KBR office building downtown, I was met by the human resource representative who introduced me to Ray Rodon, who was the senior leader at the KBR organization mentioned on the phone. As I walked into Ray's office, I, and immediately noticed a map of Kuwait and Iraq on his wall. That's when I realized this job was going to be different from what I had imagined.

Before the interview began, Ray introduced himself as the Deputy Program Manager supporting the LOGCAP III program.

Chapter 1 The Decision

I later learned that the Army established the LOGCAP (Logistics Civil Augmentation Program) in 1985, to preplan for the use of civilian contractors to perform selected services overseas to augment Army forces." I had no previous idea about LOGCAP or any civilian operation supporting the U.S. military. I grew up near Keesler Air Force base and had several friends that were children of Air Force personnel. Most important, as mentioned, my father-in-law was a veteran with a long service record extending from World War II to Korea and Vietnam—part of the greatest generation.

Ray kicked off the discussion with an overview of the position and, most importantly, confirmed that it would be based in Kuwait. My mind immediately raced— "Kuwait? What the f---?" I remained composed as Ray continued describing the role. He was somewhat vague, explaining that it was a senior leadership position supporting the transportation of military supplies from Kuwait to various locations within both Kuwait and Iraq. Again, my mind screamed, "Iraq? What the f---?"

As Ray pointed at the map of Iraq and Kuwait on his wall, detailing supply locations, I found myself in a daze. The only thoughts running through my mind were, "Iraq? Kuwait? No f'ing way," and, more importantly, "Lana is going to say 'No f'ing way.'"

After Ray finished, I asked politely, "Is the position in Kuwait or Dubai? The recruiter said Dubai." Ray quickly clarified that the position was in Kuwait and explained that the LOGCAP III contract was a Department of Defense initiative awarded to KBR. The current leader of the supply chain operation was leaving in December 2003—just weeks away.

We continued the interview, and at the end, Ray asked if I was interested in the position. While Kuwait and Iraq weren't outright deal-breakers, I had serious concerns. I told Ray I would need 48 hours to discuss the opportunity with my wife. He seemed to expect that response but stressed the urgency of the decision to ensure a smooth transition.

If I recall correctly, the interview was in mid-October 2003. As I left, my mind raced with thoughts of Kuwait and Iraq. Do I really want to do this? What will Lana think? Actually, I already knew.

When I returned to the hotel room, I suggested we go to dinner so I could explain everything. Over dinner, I laid out the details of the position and its location in Kuwait. Lana's initial reaction? "Hell no."

But as we talked through the opportunity, the compensation, and, most importantly, the chance to support our military, she agreed to at least consider it. After consulting with friends and family, she reluctantly gave her blessing.

Over the next twenty-four hours, we continued discussing various challenges the position would bring—how she would manage with two teenage boys at home, what we would tell them, and how we could lean on friends and family for support. We also reached out to friends with spouses working overseas for insight and spoke to our respective families.

To no one's surprise, my father-in-law was fully supportive, and for the most part, my parents were as well. Our closest friends in McKinney reassured us that they would help as much as possible. One close friend, Rob, even stained our backyard wooden fence while I was away. Thirty years later, Rob remains a close friend. That level of support meant a lot. In the end, Lana reluctantly agreed, and I made the decision to say 'yes.'

I contacted Ray (Houston Ray) and confirmed that I would accept the role. They made me an offer the next day. I was initially surprised by the base salary, as it seemed more modest than the figures that had initially piqued my interest. However, the KBR Human Resources representative explained that "uplift" was a combination of foreign service bonuses, area differential pay, and hazard pay, which made the total compensation significantly higher.

Chapter 1 The Decision

Additionally, the role was compensated on an hourly basis, with forty hours as the base and a required minimum of eighty-four hours per week—seven twelve-hour days. Any time over forty hours was paid at time-and-a-half. With that structure, my total compensation was well into the six figures.

They also informed me that there would be an orientation session in Houston at the end of October, and I would be flying to Kuwait on November 3rd, with an official start date of November 5th.

Within weeks, we were preparing for a new chapter in our lives. As I reassured Lana that everything would be okay, I could only hope that I truly believed it myself.

CHAPTER 2
ORIENTATION

The Drive to Houston with Lana

During the drive from our home in McKinney, Texas, to Houston—a journey that took four or five hours—Lana and I found ourselves deep in conversation, grappling with uncertainty. We were both struggling to imagine how this new chapter would unfold, short- or long-term. In hindsight, we may have been a little naive in trying to assess the potential risks.

We agreed to take things one step at a time. As a dedicated, passionate, and loyal leader and team member, I committed to giving it one year and then reassessing. While the compensation was important in the short term, it wasn't our only motivation. Lana spoke about our family and our long-term goals, reminding me not to focus solely on the mission or the money. She encouraged me to keep our future together in perspective—our children, potential grandchildren, immediate family, and close friends. These were the people who had stood by us through thick and thin—the joyful moments and the hardest ones.

We had started our personal journey together at a very young age, and we reminded ourselves that in many ways, our lives were just beginning. "Think of the future," she kept saying.

That drive also gave me time to reflect on my professional path. After college, I'd had only a vague idea of what I wanted to do. My first job taught me the fundamentals of leadership and launched me into the world of logistics. Now, as I stood on the brink of a potentially life-changing position, I found myself reflecting: Would I have done anything differently? What would a different path have meant for Lana, our kids, or me? Did I have regrets?

I didn't think so. I knew I approached work in a very specific way that motivated me—driven by a deep passion for people. Sometimes that passion showed up as frustration or intense emotion. It wasn't a detriment to the organizations I'd served, but it occasionally rubbed people the wrong way. Would that passion be a problem in this radically different environment?

When the long drive ended, we checked into the Greenspoint Marriott Hotel, just north of downtown Houston. KBR had effectively taken over the entire hotel for an extended period to conduct training, meetings, and orientation sessions for the thousands hired to support the LOGCAP III contract. My segment of the orientation was scheduled to last four and a half days.

Orientation

I was told the presentations would cover operations, personnel, leadership, military and Muslim culture, rules of engagement, infrastructure, living conditions, and threat levels.

As we arrived and checked in, I immediately noticed the incredible diversity of the group. It was a vivid slice of America—and beyond. "Diverse" didn't begin to describe us. The crowd was also much larger than I'd expected.

Chapter 2 Orientation

Several of the other senior staff held roles equivalent to mine, leading camp operations in locations like Baghdad, or what was commonly known as "The Green Zone." Truck drivers and front-line staff were also in attendance and represented the majority of the attendees. While we were united by the same mission, we came from different walks of life, with varying personal goals.

Another layer of diversity came from those who had previously worked overseas, often for KBR in post-Balkans conflict zones. Some of these individuals thrived on the adventure, the pay, and the chance to live abroad, following contracts wherever the demand took them.

Many attendees were assigned to camp management, responsible for services on U.S. military bases in Kuwait, Iraq, and Afghanistan. Think of these camps as self-contained cities. Like domestic bases, they needed to provide everything for the soldiers and support personnel—housing, food, sanitation, and more. KBR was responsible for it all, not just logistics, but construction and facility maintenance, too.

In other words, we were all about to become part of the U.S. military machine, one way or another.

What we all shared was uncertainty. KBR and Halliburton had participated in previous LOGCAP contracts, but never on this scale. Civilians were being embedded with military units for "peacetime" operations in combat zones. The complexity was staggering. Even under normal circumstances, the situation would have been borderline chaotic. But these weren't normal circumstances—this was a rapidly expanding operation, hastily assembled to meet urgent needs.

I began learning more about the history of Halliburton and KBR. Halliburton's roots stretched back to World War I, originally a pioneer in oil services. Over time, it had become a global force. After Operation Desert Storm in 1991, Halliburton earned recognition for extinguishing over 700 oil well fires left in Kuwait by Saddam Hussein's forces. Not long after, Defense Secretary Dick Cheney commissioned Halliburton's construction arm, Brown & Root, to study the use of private contractors alongside the military—though I wouldn't learn that until later.

What I did know was that Cheney became Halliburton's CEO in 1995. Under his leadership, the company merged M.W. Kellogg and Brown & Root in 1998 to form KBR—Kellogg Brown & Root. Now, as Vice President of the United States, Cheney had long since left Halliburton—but we were heading to the Middle East to work for the very company he had helped reshape.

In the days to come, I learned just how vast KBR's role had become. They weren't just managing transportation—they were hiring 20,000 people over two years to relocate, feed, house, and care for staff in the Middle East. It was the equivalent of assembling a military division from scratch.

The next morning at the Marriott, I said goodbye to Lana and began orientation, trying to keep a low profile. I wanted to blend in, to be just another team member. As a people-focused leader, I believed I could learn more if folks didn't know who I was right away. And sure enough, in just a few days, I began to get a real sense of what lay ahead. We had 300+ people from all over the country gathered in one place.

The group included both men and women, and the after-hours social scene was lively. Alcohol was flowing, and certain extra-curriculars were clearly taking place. That wasn't unusual for the time, but it was a little concerning considering the seriousness of the mission. Some attendees didn't make it through orientation—those who didn't take it seriously were quickly weeded out.

The formal sessions covered everything from organizational structure and operational goals to leadership, military infrastructure, and cultural training. There was a heavy emphasis on understanding Muslim culture and respecting local customs—we were, after all, trying to win hearts and minds, not create new enemies.

Chapter 2 Orientation

We also received detailed information about personnel needs, living conditions, threat levels, and mission expectations. At that time, overall threat levels were low. I used to say, "We kicked the ant hill, and the ants haven't made their way back yet." It was a simple, comforting analogy—but as we all know, that would soon change. And ants bite.

By Day 3, my anonymity was up. A senior KBR leader discovered I was there and immediately pulled me aside. "Mr. Richard, we're sorry—we should have known you were here. You should have let us know." I assured him I wasn't offended. I valued the chance to experience the orientation from the perspective of the front-line team.

Still, from that point on, I was pulled into more senior-level sessions. Word spread quickly that I was the Project Leader for the Theater Transportation Mission (TTM). I didn't yet fully grasp the scope of TTM, but I knew it was a major supply chain operation supporting military efforts in Kuwait and Iraq. Now that people knew who I was, I became "that" person—eyes followed me, whispers circulated.

Some team members began approaching me with questions and concerns. They were looking for reassurance. My answer was always honest: "I'm in the same position as you—uncertain, eager, and unsure of what's ahead. I'm here to learn, and I hope to succeed in supporting this mission."

I reminded them that this was an opportunity to serve the military—an honor and a serious responsibility.

As I continued to embed myself in the organization, I realized just how much I had to learn. I was both the boss and the trainee. One of the biggest challenges was cultural. Many of the staff were ex-military—officers and enlisted alike. In military terms, my role was roughly equivalent to a colonel, and I reported to retired generals. But those reporting to me came from all levels of military experience. Even though we were civilians, military habits and expectations still lingered, shaping perceptions and interactions.

This complex personnel mix was part of why I was moved away from the general sessions—so I could be situated among the "officers," in a sense.

Around this time, I committed to leaning into my hands-on leadership style. I believed it could make the difference in transforming this diverse crowd into a confident, unified team. While I still had plenty to learn, my priority was to help others close skill gaps, build confidence, and develop a shared sense of mission.

TTM would eventually include over 2,000 staff members, including third-country nationals (TCNs) from all over the world. Some had exposure to U.S. workplace culture—many did not. Language skills varied. Most of the people I'd be leading were heading into unfamiliar territory—both culturally and geographically.

I had navigated many work environments and leadership challenges before, and I felt ready. But I knew this would be the most demanding—and potentially rewarding—professional experience of my life. My background would help, but my leadership approach would have to evolve. This wasn't a 9-to-5 job. We were far from home, far from our usual support systems, and I had to be constantly alert. Others would depend on my judgment. Projecting uncertainty wasn't an option. No matter my internal doubts, I had to radiate calm and decisiveness. Anything less could hurt morale—or worse.

And I couldn't forget that I was a civilian in a military operation, without military experience. These men and women had lived in a world of structure, hierarchy, and rules. I had to find my own way to match their discipline—with a mix of polish and grit. This would be the ultimate test of everything I'd learned about leadership.

I found myself repeating the words of Gene Kranz, the Apollo 13 flight director: "Failure is not an option."

Chapter 2 Orientation

Putting Things in Perspective

That was the big picture—the thoughts I turned over in my mind deliberately some of the time, and subconsciously, all the time. But there were plenty of other things happening during this life-changing period. Much like an actual military induction, we were being prodded constantly, both figuratively and literally.

As the orientation neared completion, I had become something of a high-priority individual. Dedicated KBR personnel were assigned to me throughout days three and four, walking me through a lengthy punch list of things I needed to know, understand, and be prepared to act on. That was the prodding. What I didn't know—what no one warned me about—was the poking. Vaccinations.

Seven of them. Seven separate needles piercing my arm. And considering my lifelong fear of needles, this became my first real test of strength and willpower. I asked the medical staff to let me be alone during the process—I wasn't sure I wouldn't pass out. I managed to get through it but had to lie on a medical bed for 10 to 15 minutes afterward, just to steady myself. All the little sore spots they left behind didn't exactly help my mood.

Fortunately, the long, intense days ended with some precious downtime in the evenings, and I was grateful to spend that time with Lana.

Most nights, we'd get away from the Greenspoint Marriott and find a quiet Mexican restaurant somewhere nearby. We'd sip margaritas, talk honestly, and try to make sense of what the next several months would look like. We tried to think it through—not just for me, but for both of us. She was about to step into the new, daunting world of single parenting. I might only be a phone call away, but we both knew that wasn't the same as being there, especially when you're separated by continents and time zones.

We were both facing steep learning curves and personal challenges.

I did my best to assure her that everything would be okay. I promised we would visit each other as often as we could. At that time, I didn't yet fully understand the Rest and Relaxation (R&R) policy or the tax-related rules that would affect how and when we could reunite. I just knew I'd call her every day. Most importantly, I promised I'd stay safe.

We shared our thoughts, our love, and yes—our tears. We had been a close and successful team for so long that even contemplating this dramatic shift in our dynamic felt deeply uncomfortable. I found myself quietly questioning the decision again, though I rarely voiced it out loud. Still, I believed this was a professional opportunity I couldn't afford to pass up. In some ways, it felt like a call-up to the major leagues.

It was also a chance to support our military—something I had long respected. In addition to my father-in-law, I knew many veterans and active-duty service members. I had sometimes regretted not serving myself. Taking on this mission felt like a way to contribute, a way to support those who had answered the call. And it gave me a sense of pride that, in some small way, I was finally doing my part.

On the third day in Houston, it was time for Lana to return home. I would remain one more day, preparing to travel to Kuwait. As we said our difficult goodbye, Lana clung to me and said once again, "Don't go. Please don't go."

I held her tightly and replied, "It will be OK. Trust that I love you from the bottom of my heart—and that love will keep us strong."

We both cried. I tried to hold it together. As she walked away, I knew our lives were about to change forever. I felt a strange blend of fear and anticipation. Was I ready? At least I thought I was.

Chapter 2 Orientation

What the next twelve months would bring was entirely unknown. At that moment, the future seemed like a swirl of hazy images—a faraway desert, documents and plans, satellite maps and logistical reports I'd been poring over for days.

But I kept telling myself: *I was ready… right?*

CHAPTER 3
ARRIVAL AND INTRODUCTIONS

During the long flight from Dallas-Fort Worth to Kuwait, I was deep in thought about what I was getting into. Would my leadership approach work as it had before, or would it need to change? Who could I trust in this brand-new environment? What would things look like in the first 30, 60, or 90 days? I ran through countless scenarios, imagined conversations with people I hadn't yet met, then repeated the process to reassure myself I was ready for anything.

I knew that showing weakness or vulnerability wasn't an option. As I'd come to understand, this was an operation—and an organization—that demanded a blend of professional skill, personal strength, and unshakable confidence. Everyone relied on one another, including me, to perform their roles effectively. Most of us were in unfamiliar territory, and few had worked together before. Everyone would need to build confidence—not just in themselves, but in the team—and conveying that confidence was part of my responsibility.

Unlike Texas, where the job parts were familiar, where my roles had differed but shared a common foundation, this was something entirely new. The fear of the unknown started to creep in. I had to convince myself that I had the leadership skills to succeed. More importantly, this was my chance to prove it—to myself. As I reflected on my career, my experiences, the highs and the lows, I felt a growing sense of strength and resolve. I truly believed I could meet this challenge and evolve into what the role demanded: a no-nonsense, confident, and decisive leader.

Of course, while having all these internal conversations, I was also literally in flight—most of the time, anyway—and occasionally dealing with frustrations on the ground.

The Lufthansa flight was long and uncomfortable, with seats that felt like I was sitting on a stack of bricks. I had some unkind thoughts about German concepts of creature comfort. We had an eight-hour layover in Frankfurt, a sprawling, clean airport that somehow managed to be both modern and inhospitable. It lacked seating, and there were few options for food or refreshment. I napped as best I could—on rigid seats and even on the floor—and the sleep deprivation began to take its toll.

When it was finally time to board the flight to Kuwait, I couldn't believe it when airport security confiscated my fingernail clipper—buried deep in a trouser pocket. In carefully enunciated English, they explained that the tiny built-in file was sharp enough to be considered a potential weapon. They clearly weren't taking any chances.

At the time, it seemed ridiculous. In retrospect—after everything I'd soon experience with *actual* dangerous weapons in Iraq—it became almost laughable.

Leaving behind the familiar "Western" world of Frankfurt, it took only six more hours to deliver us to a strange new reality: Kuwait. The aircraft, luggage systems, and a few other small details looked familiar enough, but that was just our minds clinging to anything recognizable as the unfamiliar rushed in. The smells

Chapter 3   Arrival and Introductions

were different. The sun was harsher. The air was drier—baked to a brittle crispness I had never experienced, even in a Texas summer.

As I moved through security in Kuwait, I was met by a man holding a sign with my name. He was friendly and eager to help. A logistics manager with the TTM organization, he seemed ready to launch into his own version of the company's state of affairs. After a 17-hour trip and a 9-hour time change, all I could think was, *just get me to my living quarters*. We could deal with everything else tomorrow.

But he was clearly in "debrief and download" mode, launching into a monologue about everything wrong with the organization and what he thought needed fixing. I wasn't in a state to absorb any of it. I tuned him out, thinking, *I'll have time to organize my thoughts and assess everything soon enough*. He kept talking until I finally cut in, firmly: "OK, I got you. Let's start tomorrow and go from there."

I had no clear expectations for the living conditions, other than what was vaguely described during orientation. So, when we arrived, I braced for the worst. But I was pleasantly surprised. The accommodations were in a resort-style hotel that housed many of the KBR leadership and administrative staff based in Kuwait. I was assigned a private room, hotel-style—nice, if not quite luxurious. In the moment, it felt like a shimmering oasis.

To the gentleman helping with my bags, I said I'd see him at 6:00 a.m. But he informed me that I'd be meeting my predecessor for breakfast at that time. Fine. Sleep came quickly—though not nearly enough—and the next morning snapped everything back into focus. While many staff were crammed into multi-room accommodations with four or five people per unit, senior leaders like me were afforded private quarters.

I met my predecessor for breakfast as scheduled. From what I recall, the conversation was fairly generic. It was clear he was burned out—deep in a "short-timer's" mindset and focused solely on getting the hell out. The transition was planned to last two weeks—not much time, considering the size, scope, and complexity of the operation. Sensing my surprise, he explained that he'd planned to leave in October, but the company had struggled to fill the role. He gave KBR until the end of November, which he apparently considered a major sacrifice. Now, as he put it, "I'm getting the hell out."

Had I not spent the entire flight psyching myself up, I might have been more rattled. Instead, I shrugged it off and reassured myself that I was well equipped to handle what lay ahead. Still, his defeated tone was hard to ignore.

Was everyone here feeling this way?

With approximately 20,000 people scattered across Kuwait, Iraq, and Afghanistan, LOGCAP III operated like a corporation within a corporation. Kuwait City, the capital and largest city in Kuwait, had a population of around three million—roughly seventy percent of the country's total. It featured a relatively robust infrastructure, with large office buildings and sprawling apartment complexes. Many of those apartment buildings housed third-country nationals (TCNs), typically blue-collar workers employed by contractors for manual labor jobs, both within Kuwait and across various roles supporting LOGCAP III and other contractor missions, including truck drivers. From what I could observe, the place was active and had a strong sense of purpose.

KBR wasn't the only contractor operating in support of the military, either. There was a real buzz around the region. On the surface, it might have seemed a little sleepy, but beneath that was a fast-moving engine of activity—people working and thinking in "New York minutes."

Now it was time to meet the customers—the Army folks.

The drive to Camp Arifjan was an eye-opener. Sand, hills, and camels. I'd never seen a camel in the wild before and, for a few drifting moments, I felt like a tourist. Camp Arifjan, the largest

Chapter 3 Arrival and Introductions

U.S. military base in Kuwait, was about an hour south of Kuwait City, near the Persian Gulf coast. When we arrived, it felt oddly familiar. Having grown up and worked at Keesler AFB in Biloxi, Mississippi, I knew that most military bases had a way of looking and feeling alike. Even here, thousands of miles from home, "Camp" still meant a little piece of America—albeit temporary and perpetually under construction. Tents, metal buildings, trailers, and heavy equipment filled the landscape.

After the Khobar Towers bombing in Saudi Arabia in 1996, the U.S. Army made the decision to move operations from Camp Doha near Basrah to a more secure location. In July 1999, the Kuwaiti government began construction on what would become Camp Arifjan.

When we arrived at the TTM office, I found it housed in a cramped 20'x10' trailer with about 10 people jammed inside. My desk was a small space right in the middle of the chaos. I wasn't expecting luxury, but my first impression was that I'd been demoted to the shipping dock. Ten people on computers, talking at once—it was hardly a productive environment. My second thought was, *this should be interesting... and where the hell is the rest of the support staff?*

I learned that our phones ran through a satellite system with a Houston, Texas, area code. That meant I could call friends and family in the Houston area like I was calling from next door. My brother Leo lived—and still lives—there, as did several close friends. They became my sounding board during those early days. For international calls outside of Houston, we used prepaid calling cards loaded with several hours of talk time. I used mine often to call Lana, as we'd agreed to speak daily—no matter what. They were in this pressure cooker with me.

I was introduced to several of my direct reports and support staff. Three of them—James, Ray, and Art—quickly became my trusted inner circle. I called them, affectionately, the Three Amigos. (That was also the title of a comedy film that came out around the time Lana and I got married. Though, honestly, I can't remember if we ever saw it. Those early years were a blur.)

Though technically subordinates, the intensity of the environment transformed these men into my brothers-in-arms. James would become the number two in command of the TTM Kuwait operation. A retired Sergeant Major—the highest-ranking non-commissioned officer in the Army—and former Drill Sergeant, James carried natural authority. He also had a deep, instinctive respect for the chain of command. His military training had taught him that in a crisis, everyone had to know their role and execute it without hesitation. He served as the Deputy Project Manager (DPM) for Kuwait.

Ray (British Ray), a Logistics Director, managed procurement and purchasing functions. Hailing from the U.K., Ray introduced me to the daily ritual of hot tea and cookies. Every morning in Kuwait, he brought them to my desk—a small act that helped keep me, and the team, steady and ready to face whatever came next.

Art served as our liaison officer (LNO)—formally, the Senior Liaison Director. His job was to work directly with the military, maintaining communication with senior leaders and coordinating across projects and operations. Art was our "eyes and ears" at the Tactical Operations Center (TOC) at Camp Arifjan.

I met the rest of the support staff and joined the team's morning meeting. Then came another curveball I hadn't seen coming. As mentioned, James would eventually assume the DPM role. What I didn't know was that the current DPM was also leaving—by the end of December. Given the size and complexity of the operation, that was yet another *"What the f'ing hell?"* moment. My predecessor informed me that someone *was supposed* to have briefed me on the transition. That clearly hadn't happened. To make matters worse, the current DPM was already in Iraq at Camp Anaconda, supporting a similar transition there. So where exactly did that leave us here?

Chapter 3 Arrival and Introductions

It was déjà vu of the worst kind.

This was a senior leadership position within the TTM organization—one I hadn't been involved in hiring for, but one I heavily depended on. Camp Anaconda, located about 40 miles north of Baghdad, was originally named Al-Bakr Air Base, after Iraq's former president who preceded Saddam Hussein. The U.S. captured it in 2003 and renamed it Camp Anaconda. I couldn't help but wonder where the name came from. A snake? Really? But there wasn't time for idle speculation.

What I quickly learned was that Camp Anaconda was the second-largest base in Iraq and home to one of the busiest airports in the world. If the name "Anaconda" didn't catch your attention, the soldiers—and soon everyone else—had nicknamed it "Mortaritaville," thanks to the constant mortar and rocket propelled grenades (RPG) fire lobbed at the camp by insurgents. Having lived there later for four months, I can say with certainty: the name fit.

But I'm getting ahead of myself.

The rest of the day was filled with Q&A sessions with my predecessor and an overview of the organization and its operations. My world was now split in two: nights at a reasonably comfortable "resort," filled with a mostly male crowd whose interests centered around sleep, dining facility meals (DFAC), and the minimal creature comforts the region could offer—and days spent inside a hot, crowded trailer filled with KBR staff, laptops, and nonstop activity.

As we traveled around Kuwait and visited additional sites, I began to get a feel for the people and the culture. More of that *"We're not in Kansas anymore"* feeling came from watching the Kuwaitis in their own environment. One moment particularly stands out: we were stopped at a red light, and my predecessor—an unrepentant chain smoker—lit up a cigarette. It was Ramadan, the Muslim holy month, a time marked by fasting and strict abstinence from tobacco, sexual activity, and other behaviors deemed sinful.

Any violation of these rules was taken very seriously. Ramadan is a deeply spiritual period, focused on prayer and devotion to the Quran.

At night, festive tents decorated with what looked like Christmas lights sprang up across the desert. These were designated spaces for post-fast celebrations. But during the day, the restrictions were clear.

When a Kuwaiti man in the car next to us noticed the cigarette, he immediately rolled down his window and told my predecessor to stop. He complied without argument, then turned to me and said, "We're in their world."

It was a lesson in awareness and respect.

Temperatures frequently soared to 120 degrees, and sandstorms whipped through like clouds of talcum powder, infiltrating every crevice of your body and gear. I quickly understood why masks, long sleeves, and goggles weren't just recommended—they were essential. Dressing in full coverage might've been uncomfortable, but it was absolutely necessary.

The differences between the haves and the have-nots were starker and more visible than anything I'd seen back in the U.S. If you were a Kuwaiti citizen—especially if you were part of the extensive Royal Family—you were supported by the government with housing, education, income, and more. The Al Sabah family, which has ruled since 1752, was known by the time of my stay for its significant investments in U.S. stocks, oil, and real estate. At that time, it was ranked the second wealthiest royal family in the world, with an estimated net worth of $360 billion.

And yet, in this incredibly wealthy country, the actual labor was performed by contractors—many of them with very little—who carried out the bulk of the manual work.

As I began to settle into my first week in Kuwait, I noticed more than just the Three Amigos. It quickly became clear that not everything was operating as it should. I began to form opinions—quiet

Chapter 3 Arrival and Introductions

suspicions, really—about certain staff and their roles in the organization. At first, it was just a gut feeling.

There was definitely a "good ol' boy" culture in play. Many of the staff had worked together on other LOGCAP projects, either with KBR or other contractors. It was a bit incestuous—cliques of people who knew each other from "way back when," speaking in their own shorthand, and often more focused on surviving and securing the next assignment than supporting the mission. Most of them were just doing what they needed to get by. They didn't want to rock the boat.

That attitude was understandable—but it wasn't helpful. For those of us who took seriously the commitment to "support the troops," it raised a question: Would these people actually step up in an emergency or bear their share of the burden?

That first week was a whirlwind of meetings, introductions, questions, and intense conversations. After several days of meet-and-greet sessions, briefings, social events, and getting the lay of the land, I began to feel like I was starting to understand the structure, the players, and the landscape.

But meetings with senior members of the KBR LOGCAP and Halliburton teams—including the LOGCAP III Project leadership—brought with them new insights, and more than a few surprises.

I had plenty of questions for my predecessor. What exactly was the organizational structure? What was the chain of command? What were our overarching mission objectives? Who were my direct reports? Where were our staff based, in Kuwait and in Iraq? Who were our military contacts? Some of the answers were helpful. Others... not so much. One answer hit me like a bolt of lightning: "This position is domiciled in Iraq."

Another *"what the f'ing hell"* moment—one of many that would follow.

"I was told the position was based in Kuwait with periodic visits to Iraq," I said, trying to stay calm. "No," he replied. "The position is transitioning to the Iraq Logistics Hub at Anaconda."

He explained that the primary mission had shifted to supporting the Iraq logistics operation and that the TTM Project Manager was now based out of Camp Anaconda. After the initial shock wore off, I began reorganizing my thoughts. But another question immediately surfaced: *What do I tell Lana?*

Wanting to protect her—and maybe a little seduced by the talk of mission-critical work and its importance—I broke from our usual communication style. I decided not to tell her everything. I had a job to do, and I told myself that everything would be fine. When we spoke, I shared the usual day-to-day details, but I left out the crucial fact that I was now going to be based in Iraq.

And then, as if that weren't enough, he casually added, "We're both traveling to Anaconda next week for introductions."

One big adjustment after another. Once again, not knowing exactly what to expect, I collected my thoughts and absorbed the information. I contacted Houston Ray to get his take. He was unaware of the change and simply advised patience, describing it as a "fluid operation." I wasn't sure "fluid" was the right word—but surprise or not, this was a big shift.

As we continued reviewing the organization that week, I discovered that there wasn't even an organization chart to give a sense of the structure or the reporting lines. I quickly made that one of my top priorities. Then came another curveball: the infamous "Kuwaiti Crud."

After a few days, I came down with what staff told me was a common stomach virus that seemed to affect nearly everyone newly arrived in Kuwait. Without going into graphic detail, I spent two miserable days bouncing between my desk and the restroom. The crew thought it was funny. I didn't. But it was just one more item on the growing list of chaos.

Chapter 3 Arrival and Introductions

In a weird way, it helped. I'd gained too much weight in my previous role—too many fast-food burgers and fries. The Crud knocked five pounds off me instantly. Silver lining, I guess.

I used that moment as a reset and recommitted myself to a fitness program. There wasn't much else to do beyond eat, sleep, and work. I lost twenty pounds over the next two months. I don't want to turn this into a fitness bio, but the changes were real. I shifted to two meals a day, focused on the job, stayed off alcohol almost entirely, and made health a priority.

There were a few positives—like meeting some fascinating characters as I traveled around to different sites in Kuwait. But with 20,000 hires in a short span of time, you were bound to run into a few bad apples. My instincts remained in overdrive.

As I engaged more deeply with the TTM leadership, it became clear to them—and to me—that I wasn't part of the "good ol' boy" network. And that things were about to change.

I didn't have the luxury of deciding whether to be a no-nonsense, hard-nosed leader. The organization *needed* structure and control. Without it, we were inviting financial problems—or worse. Word spread quickly that I was on a mission. Like most leaders in high-pressure environments, I began identifying confidants—the people I could truly trust.

One early red flag was the Transportation Manager. From what I gathered, he believed he was responsible for transportation across the entire TTM mission—or at least, he acted like it. When I visited his "office" in Kuwait, my Spidey senses started tingling.

Vendor hats and paraphernalia were scattered everywhere. I asked him, "Why is there vendor merchandise in your office?"

He replied that KBR's procurement team conducted vendor meetings there. My follow-up: "Is that proper protocol?"

He didn't have a direct answer. Just a shrug and the old line: "That's how it's always been."

"Well," I said, "not anymore."

That situation would continue to develop. But right away, I knew something wasn't right, and I needed to dig deeper into his operation. Then came yet another jolt.

I had been attending meetings for several days, including those with military personnel, when I realized something critical: no one had processed my security clearance. Another *"What the F...?"* moment.

This wasn't a small issue. The military thrives on structure and protocol. Both civilian and military personnel must undergo vetting and receive the appropriate security clearance—typically Secret or Top Secret—based on their duties. Without one, I was essentially useless in any official military meeting or planning session. And getting cleared isn't an overnight process. Back in the States, it can take months.

Meeting senior military officials—generals, colonels, and others—I quickly realized that earning their respect was going to be both a challenge and a necessity. I was a civilian, with no prior military experience, and now I didn't even have the clearance badge to prove I was part of the team. Their looks said it all: *How could KBR send a senior supply chain leader to run the largest mission in theater without any military background—and without a security clearance?*

Thankfully, KBR moved quickly. I'm pretty sure they had to go all the way up to the Secretary of Defense's office to make it happen, but my clearance was issued in January 2004. Finally, I was able to participate in military briefings and planning sessions. I began catching up on everything I had missed—on both the mission itself and the broader military picture.

What I can say is that the experience was truly eye-opening and demanded a new level of awareness and acumen. It reinforced, more than ever, the critical importance of discipline, respect, and protocol—not just for KBR's success, but for mine as well.

CHAPTER 4

OVERVIEW, CONFUSION AND DISORDER

With all—or at least most—of the information now available to me, I began to fully grasp the scale and complexity of the Theater Transportation Mission (TTM). We were responsible for managing the largest civilian supply chain operation supporting the U.S. military anywhere in the world at that time. This included airfield operations, postal service support, trucking, theater movement control, classified heavy equipment transport, yard and fueling operations, water and ice distribution, and more. It was clear this was going to be a massive challenge. Our organization was new—and so was I. No wonder the military staff were skeptical.

As I'd already discovered, there was no real organizational structure in place. No defined protocols. No clear chain of command. No detailed roles and responsibilities. Back in the U.S., those would have been expected—even for a routine operation where the worst-case scenario was a dissatisfied customer. But here, where lives were at stake, such chaos was unacceptable. It was a flashing red warning sign.

Was this a failure on my predecessor's part? Or had higher-level decisions—mission changes, resource shifts—undermined his efforts before he even had a chance? And if that was true, what would stop the same thing from happening to me?

I didn't know yet. But what I did know was that I had to create structure: protocols, clear roles, responsibilities, business requirements—and ensure that everyone understood and followed them. I also expected resistance—especially from the more entrenched, self-protecting members of the KBR staff.

I remained in Kuwait through December while James and I transitioned into our new roles. During this time, I began to feel more settled. I was no longer the new guy. I recognized faces, understood personalities, and started to build confidence in the road ahead. At the same time, though, threat levels in Iraq were escalating.

We soon received the sobering news that one of our truck drivers had been killed in hostile action. Our convoys—transporting supplies across and within Iraq—were starting to come under attack.

This wasn't entirely unexpected, but it was certainly more than Lana or I had anticipated when we first discussed this opportunity over Mexican food and margaritas back home.

Conversations with senior military leaders quickly shifted to the need for enhanced force protection. Force protection is when the military embeds soldiers driving fully armed military vehicles into civilian convoys for military support and protection. Civilians were not allowed to be armed or carry any type of weapons. Understandably, they had their own escalating priorities, and providing resources to protect contractors like us likely hadn't figured into their original plans. The discussions were often tense, but we eventually pushed through changes to the rules of engagement (ROE) and secured commitments for convoy security.

Chapter 4 Overview, Confusion and Disorder

It was agreed that the Army would provide force protection for KBR convoys running from Camp Cedar north to Baghdad and Anaconda, and from Anaconda to other bases. We also used Camp Scania, a small base approximately 125 miles from Camp Cedar as a relay point for cargo including eight of the ten military supply classes: Class I through X. Class V (ammunition) and Class VIII (medical supplies) were excluded from our contract. Class III—JP8 fuel used for military vehicles—was the highest volume, representing about seventy percent of TTM's mission volume. Fuel convoys traveled as dedicated units; other supplies were shipped on mixed flatbed convoys.

These supply classes represented the heavy, high-volume essentials—but the mission's scope didn't stop there. We also managed all postal services (receiving, sorting, transporting, and delivering), movement control (scheduling and coordinating the movement of personnel, equipment, and supplies), airfield operations (inter- and intra-theater routing), heavy equipment transport (tanks, armored vehicles), vehicle recovery, potable and non-potable water supply, and—believe it or not—ice. Yes, ice was a hot commodity in Iraq.

We also handled operations for camp equipment and managed several staging yards. You get the picture—this was a huge, moving operation with more moving parts than most people could possibly imagine. It was like rebuilding a major section of U.S. infrastructure from scratch—but with limited resources, tight timelines, rudimentary systems, and the looming danger of insurgency.

Operations were based in Kuwait and extended across Iraq, covering numerous forward operating bases (FOBs). Our primary supply hubs or convoy staging areas were at Navistar in Kuwait, Camp Cedar in southern Iraq, and Camp Anaconda in the north. Most of KBR's over-the-road (OTR) transport equipment—trucks, flatbeds, and tankers—were based at these hubs.

In traditional supply chain terms, it was a hub-and-spoke model. Ironically, the military had pioneered many of the supply chain principles that civilian industries later adopted—automotive, retail, consumer goods, manufacturing—most rely on hub-and-spoke systems today. The big difference? In the military, hubs are supplied based on strategic and tactical battlefield needs. Efficiency and asset utilization take a backseat to mission readiness.

Sometimes the military would order us to move empty flatbeds and tankers between hubs—just to ensure readiness for the next wave of supplies. From a civilian supply chain perspective, this broke every rule in the book. But the goal wasn't efficiency. The goal was battlefield support.

The catch? Civilians like us weren't originally supposed to be on the battlefield.

These shifting priorities challenged everything I'd learned as a civilian logistics leader. I made recommendations. I drafted proposals. I met with generals and senior officers to advocate for improvements to the transportation network model.

It was a good effort. But I wasn't going to change hundreds of years of military logistics thinking. Eventually, I had to accept the limitations and move on.

KBR's Class-8 tractors were mostly Volvos and Mercedes. Back in the States, when people think of tractor-trailers, they think of Freightliner, Peterbilt, Mack, Kenworth, or International. In the U.S., Volvo and Mercedes were viewed as luxury brands, so the optics weren't great. There was a perception that KBR had splurged on "luxury" trucks.

The reality was different. In Europe and the Middle East, Volvos and Mercedes were workhorses—their equivalent of a Peterbilt or a Mack. But they were smaller, less powerful, and ultimately less suited for the harsh conditions we were about to face. These trucks were designed for civilian logistics—not warzones. They had no armor. The drivers, too, were ill-equipped—no vests, no helmets, no protection.

Chapter 4 Overview, Confusion and Disorder

We had entered this mission under the premise of peace—rebuilding Iraq and Afghanistan. But the situation was deteriorating. And the warning lights were flashing red.

The convoy commander trucks were outfitted with GPS and communication devices, which allowed our tactical operations centers (TOC) to track movements. Supplies traveled in convoys typically averaging twenty-five trucks per with a convoy commander positioned as the leader of the convoy. These early GPS telematics systems were helpful, but far from foolproof—and nowhere near as reliable as the tech we have today.

At this point, there were approximately 2,000 TTM employees staged throughout Kuwait and Iraq. Some were already in locations that were rapidly being identified as extremely hostile and dangerous. Fallujah, for example—known as the "City of Mosques" with over 200 scattered across its geography and surrounding villages—soon became the epicenter of the terrorist resistance during the insurgency. It's likely no coincidence. An incident in April 2003, early in the war, had resulted in civilian casualties, fueling anti-American sentiment. Ultimately, U.S. forces suffered 151 deaths and more than 1,000 wounded in two major battles there.

And civilian truckers were supposed to drive through this city?

The warning signs were no longer blinking—they were flashing bright red. Those signs continued during my first weeks in Kuwait and intensified after my visit to Iraq.

Traveling to Anaconda for the first time, I got my introduction to the military term: "hurry up and wait." Even though I was considered senior staff and higher priority, the system didn't care—we all had to sign up and get on the manifest like everyone else. At the Arifjan airfield and staging area, I was greeted by long lines and rows of cots. My first thought? *What the f—?* There were a lot of those moments. A colleague reminded me, "This isn't the U.S."

I spent nearly ten hours waiting—without even the modest creature comforts of a commercial airport. In the U.S., you have a schedule. In Theater, you have a "strong maybe." Flights were on C-5s, C-17s, and C-130s. The C-130, known as the "Hercules," is a versatile workhorse—and my first military flying experience was in one, strapped into a cargo net seat alongside several young soldiers, many clearly on their first trip to Iraq as well. The fear in their eyes said everything.

We boarded via the cargo ramp in the rear, and because I was technically "moving to Iraq," I brought a few personal items with me. Even if the trip ended up being short, I wanted to be prepared. Each of us claimed a spot, buckled into our cargo nets, and braced for what would become another *what the f'ing hell* moment. I noticed an Army sergeant sitting by a side window, eyes fixed outside. That caught my attention.

As we approached Anaconda, I understood why. He was likely a weapons sergeant, responsible for operating onboard defenses—guns, cannons, and flare systems. What followed was no ordinary descent. This wasn't a commercial airline's smooth glide into the runway. This was a full spiral drop—straight down over the airfield from 15,000 to 20,000 feet. The pilot banked sharply, circling tighter and tighter, descending with every rotation. The crew scanned for threats. After several high-stress minutes, the plane pulled out of the spiral and touched down.

The entire maneuver took seven to ten minutes. During the descent, the sergeant began firing flares—our first signal that this wasn't just a drill. The insurgents had acquired heat-seeking, shoulder-fired weapons like the SA-7, SA-14, and SA-16. The flares were our best hope at distracting them. This wasn't a rollercoaster. This was real.

I'd ridden the Texas Giant at Six Flags more than once, but this was something else entirely. This wasn't amusement. It was life and death. Some of the younger soldiers were vomiting. Me? I was too horrified. I felt sick, yes, but more than anything, I was just thinking: *Get me on the ground.* When we landed, the Army sergeant allowed himself a slight grin.

Chapter 4 Overview, Confusion and Disorder

Warning signs? No—this was the real deal.

During my visit to Iraq, I got a firsthand look at the operating conditions. The accommodations were exactly what I expected—large tents, cots, cold showers when they worked, and DFACs with a no-frills menu. The food was military-grade—high protein, high carbs. Meat, potatoes, vegetables. Eggs, bacon, bread, chicken, corn, beans. The basics to keep soldiers moving. Sleep was a luxury. Between the cots, the snoring, the booms of nearby conflict, and the constant drone of helicopters, a 15-minute nap was about the best you could hope for.

I met with the current Kuwait DPM—who was then stationed in Iraq—and the recently hired Iraq DPM. The Kuwait DPM was initially standoffish, not particularly open or collaborative. I later learned he hadn't been considered for the TTM Project Manager role—and it stung. He was a seasoned leader with tenure, and the slight had clearly left a mark. Over time, however, we developed a strong professional relationship and eventually a friendship. We stayed in touch after his departure, and he came to deeply respect me and the work we did together.

I officially offered James the DPM role for Kuwait during this time. As mentioned, James—along with British Ray and Art—would become my inner circle, my most trusted advisors.

The new Iraq DPM was another story. A seasoned KBR contractor who had followed missions from one geography to the next, he struck me as… different. Something about him was off. While he appeared to be on the level, there was something unique about his demeanor that I couldn't quite put my finger on.

I also met the Flatbed and Bulk Fuel Transportation Managers. I walked into their office—a cramped trailer—and found them with their feet propped up on desks, eating MREs (meals ready to eat). First impressions count, and this was… well, another confirmation that the good ol' boy network was alive and well. I didn't have enough time to fully assess their operations, so I kept my thoughts to myself. This visit was more of a meet-and-greet—with staff and key military leadership.

But mentally, I was already making plans. This was where I believed my people skills could make a real difference.

More and more, it became clear that the success of our mission hinged on two things: culture and structure. Logistics alone was daunting—an operation of this magnitude, stretched across hostile territory, already came with a million moving parts. But now, we were dealing with serious risks to life and limb.

If I couldn't unite the "good ol' boys" and the wide-eyed newcomers, if I couldn't get them operating under a shared vision with clearly defined responsibilities, then this mission would be in trouble. And so would we.

My 60-day plan focused on establishing a clear organizational structure—complete with org charts, reporting lines, defined roles and responsibilities, and protocols to maintain control of our assets and, most importantly, our people. Working closely with the team, we developed a centralized database that tracked all equipment and personnel across the theater. It functioned as our mission control application, logging every piece of equipment, every driver, every movement—where they were going, when they left, and when they arrived.

This system became a cornerstone of our operations. It supported everything from logistics to safety to security. We finally had visibility into our most critical resources. For the first time, we knew—without ambiguity—who and what was in motion. Those first 60 days flew by. But we made real progress.

The organizational charts were distributed. Everyone could see where they fit into the bigger picture. Individual roles and responsibilities were formalized. Most importantly, we began communicating a clear vision for TTM's mission and objectives. It wasn't exactly "my way or the highway," but it was certainly "get on the highway with me or get off."

Chapter 4 Overview, Confusion and Disorder

The swift move toward professionalism elevated our credibility. Military leaders, DoD contracting officers, and corporate leaders at KBR and Halliburton began to see us differently. We weren't just filling seats—we were building something that worked.

As Lana and I had planned, we scheduled a much-needed R&R in London—our first real break since I'd arrived. I was counting down the days, excited to see her again and to just *be* with her, away from war, even if only briefly.

To make it happen, I had to peel myself away from the daily grind and get to the Kuwait airport—now a far cry from the overwhelming chaos I'd experienced as a jet-lagged new arrival. I felt like a seasoned hand now. And this time, I made sure to fly British Airways.

I arranged for Lana's direct flight and transport to the hotel in London. When she arrived, we embraced, both of us overcome with emotion. There were tears of joy, of relief, of reconnection. But no reunion goes quite according to plan.

On her flight, Lana's abscessed tooth flared up—likely triggered by the pressure changes. By the time she reached the hotel, her jaw was swollen and the pain unbearable. Over-the-counter pain meds weren't touching it. We asked the hotel staff for the nearest clinic, and as luck would have it, there was one just a few blocks away.

It was a British civilian clinic, not unlike a local urgent care in the U.S. We walked in, and she was admitted immediately. The doctor diagnosed the infection and gave her an antibiotic injection, then prescribed additional antibiotics and Vicodin to take with her.

As we approached the desk to check out, I pulled out my credit card and insurance information, preparing for a hefty bill, and hopeful they'd accept U.S. insurance. But the administrator simply said, "There's no charge."

I blinked. "Can you repeat that—and put it in writing?" She smiled and reassured me it was fine. We were U.S. citizens, and I was working for the Department of Defense. No charge. A small miracle.

Thankfully, Lana's symptoms improved quickly. We were able to enjoy the rest of our week in London. We dined at a Gordon Ramsay restaurant, visited historic landmarks, and attended the *We Will Rock You* musical—a tribute to Queen. We both loved it. It was a trip we would always remember. Lana has always been drawn to big cities, and London quickly became one of her favorites.

As the week ended, we said our goodbyes at Heathrow. What I didn't say—what I still couldn't bring myself to say—was that I had officially been assigned to Iraq. I told myself it was better left unsaid. There was no sense adding to her worry. She already carried enough. We kissed. We hugged. And I watched her go through security.

That final image of Lana stayed with me—the warmth of her smile, the curve of her lips, her radiant face. I can't recall what she was wearing. I just remember her eyes... and the way I couldn't stop watching her until she disappeared through the terminal.

I stood there, emotionally drained, preparing myself once again for Kuwait and Iraq.

And chaos.

CHAPTER 5

A HOT SEAT AND SOME COLD REALITIES

I returned to Kuwait from the trip to London with Lana feeling both refreshed and emotionally raw. The time together had been a much-needed break. We reconnected by talking about family, friends, and everything normal. It helped ease the tension I'd been carrying, and for a little while, I forgot about my impending transition to Anaconda.

I wrestled with whether to tell Lana the truth—that I was going to Iraq. But in the end, I still believed it was better left unsaid. I didn't want it hanging over our time together or weighing on her after she returned home.

Once she left, reality came rushing back. I can hardly recall the last few hours in the UK. The trip felt like borrowed time, and now it had to be paid back. I was frustrated with the overall LOGCAP situation and increasingly concerned about what lay ahead in Iraq.

On the flight back to Kuwait, my mind wouldn't stop racing. I wasn't exactly homesick—but I missed normalcy. I missed my people. I tried to disconnect from those feelings and focus on what came next, though that, too, was a guessing game with high stakes.

Oddly enough, landing in Kuwait brought a strange sense of relief. At least there, I had some control.

This was my new "home"—and it was where I could get things done. My mission now included rooting out the bad apples—those with destructive attitudes or behaviors who threatened the success of our operation.

Back in Kuwait, I focused on stabilizing and reinforcing the new structure. We were finding our rhythm. I held daily meetings with the leadership team to review progress, address concerns, and ensure alignment. I also connected with KBR's contract management, Army generals, Defense Contract Management Agency (DCMA) representatives, and other military contracting offices. These relationships were crucial. Navigating the rules, regulations, and legalities of a complex DoD contract required precision and credibility.

That bureaucratic and political legwork paid off. I earned the trust of key military and contracting leaders, and we finalized roles, responsibilities, and protocol with the Kuwait-based staff.

My transition to Iraq happened in phases, each one complicated by bureaucratic turf wars and power plays within the sprawling network of military and civilian leadership. Along the way, I made a few enemies, plenty of frenemies, and a small circle of real allies—people I could trust no matter what.

The most problematic characters were, unsurprisingly, some of the tenured KBR LOGCAP staff. Many had gained seniority through earlier contracts and seemed to believe that "experience" equated to competence. But from my perspective as a newcomer, it was obvious some of these folks were doing more harm than good. They resisted change, clung to outdated systems, and made it harder to build an effective team. So, I leaned into my role as a hard-ass—laying down rules, enforcing discipline, and pushing structure. We were going to build a real team.

But enforcing structure wasn't the only challenge. I was under constant scrutiny—from military leaders who viewed me as both a

Chapter 5 A Hot Seat and Some Cold Realities

"newbie" and a civilian outsider. And because of our murky "support-the-Army-but-not-part-of-the-Army" role, we were questioned from every angle—internally and externally.

Back home, KBR, Halliburton, and the military were all under the microscope. "Halliburton" had become a household name—and not in a good way. Media outlets and political critics were having a field day speculating about the company's cozy relationship with the DoD. All we could do was keep our heads down and focus on the job.

Of course, I didn't see my job as "just go along to get along." Coming in from the outside gave me a different perspective, and I wasn't afraid to challenge long-held assumptions, legacy systems, or inefficient processes—if they didn't make sense, I questioned them.

That said, it wasn't always easy preaching change while wearing the KBR badge. Everyone knew KBR had secured a multi-billion-dollar contract. We were expected to keep military camps functioning smoothly, and many believed we were being overpaid to do so. That led to a common refrain: *If you've been paid to do the job, why are you rocking the boat? Just get on with it.*

Every job has its challenges. I adopted a mindset that I was part of the Army command structure even though I wasn't in uniform. That meant choosing my words carefully, especially with military leadership. It often came down to: *Yes, we'll get it done. But here's how we have to do it based on our rules of engagement.*

I also became increasingly cautious about who I could trust. One unexpected bright spot came when I ran into someone I'd worked with in the civilian world. He now had a role in-theater, and we could talk shop without walking on eggshells. That kind of connection was rare—and valuable.

Meanwhile, a deeper conflict was brewing in Kuwait. Halliburton, which had acquired KBR, was starting to feel the strain. They had a major presence in the region tied to oil and gas operations, and they were a serious player in the Middle East. But we—the KBR LOGCAP contingent—were a subsidiary running a massive services contract for Uncle Sam. And while we didn't report directly to Halliburton's Middle East offices, they were "on the ground" and expected deference. Their influence complicated our work. It wasn't direct control, but it was enough second-guessing to slow us down and make an already tough job even harder. That was the big-picture tension.

On the ground, I started visiting camps to get a closer look at how the organization actually operated. My concerns grew quickly. Hot-button issues like nepotism, favoritism, and sexual harassment were surfacing. And at every level, there were ongoing questions about TTM's roles inside the military camps. The logistical challenges were enormous. But the cultural and structural challenges? Just as daunting.

Because TTM was considered an independent organization from the KBR Camp (Base) Management structure, we were in constant negotiation with KBR Camp Management teams over living quarters, conditions, infrastructure, and space allocation. There were obvious internal power struggles—not just within KBR leadership but between various factions of the operation. Many Camp Management leaders wanted to control TTM's organization and activities *within* the camps. Strangely, no one wanted to touch anything *outside* the wire. I wonder why? Like it or not, that was TTM's domain.

Turf wars happen in any organization, but amid the mounting pressure and complexity of a warzone, they felt especially absurd. Still, I worked to stay cool and pushed for what we needed. Slowly, I started to build some real collaboration with Camp Management leadership. That didn't stop the 'good ol' boy' network from trying to blow things up whenever they saw progress. Some of these guys weren't interested in teamwork. They were focused on protecting their turf and careers. To them, "collaboration" was a dirty word.

These conflicts rarely escalated into open battles, but there was a constant stream of petty skirmishes. One front was the

Chapter 5 A Hot Seat and Some Cold Realities

ever-expanding language of military jargon and acronyms. I became a quick study and could often spot people misusing terms they didn't even understand. Even the acronyms varied by branch. Each military unit had its own dialect. "Roger" was a staple, of course, but as a civilian transportation guy, my preferred sign-off was "10-4." The Camp Manager in Kuwait and I had a running joke—he was a retired Air Force pilot, so we'd end our calls with, "Goodbye, trucker" and "Goodbye, crash pilot."

I learned to navigate all this, but it was one more obstacle. If you didn't speak the lingo or weren't "one of them," it was easy to be dismissed. And being dismissed could have serious consequences.

But I wasn't easily discouraged. I'm competitive by nature, and I wasn't about to let a few bad apples derail me—or TTM. They had their good ol' boy network. I had my *Ole Miss By Damn* attitude, with a little *Don't Mess With Texas* thrown in. If they wanted to undermine us, I'd just make TTM stronger.

Over time, we built our own infrastructure and became a stand-alone operation, independent of the camp management system. Sure, we had to beg and borrow technical support from plumbers, electricians, and other trades, but we got it done. That made some folks angrier than a pack of wild dogs.

KBR executive leadership in theater kept pressuring us to "restructure" TTM. But I stayed on the offensive, holding firm to what my team and I knew was critical to our mission in the LOGCAP III operation. We were proud of what we were doing—and we were doing it well. To some, we were still the "island of misfit toys," a group of civilians who didn't just go along with the program. But we were mission-focused and resilient.

If the word *dysfunction* is popping into your head right now, you're not wrong. TTM had challenges. LOGCAP III had challenges. The entire American presence in the region had challenges. No wonder things sometimes seemed borderline crazy and definitely chaotic.

Another wrinkle came from KBR executive leadership. The senior leader over Kuwait and Iraq when I arrived was a retired colonel named John Downey. We quickly built a relationship of mutual respect and camaraderie. From my perspective, he was effective inside the organization and out. But not long after I arrived, KBR corporate decided to bring in retired generals to lead key positions. Their theory was that this would boost credibility with the military brass. I understood the logic, but it felt like they were papering over deeper problems—putting lipstick on a pig.

My concern wasn't just about appearances. I worried the civilian support mission would get buried under a top-heavy command structure full of former generals who thought in Army terms. We weren't military. We were civilians supporting a DoD operation. But the lines were starting to blur.

Fortunately, Houston Ray—the man who originally interviewed me back in Texas—also transferred into theater. He became a close confidant, someone who deeply understood the complexities of civilian life inside a military world.

Getting TTM squared away at ground level meant staying true to our values. No turning a blind eye. You could have a smoother ride by not noticing things, but I chose to see. And what I saw during my Iraq visit put everything into perspective.

The long-tenured KBR contractors were clearly in control. My first impression? It looked like the Wild West on steroids—with a side of Jack Daniels. It felt like Momma and Daddy were gone, and the kids were running the house.

There were plenty of "extracurricular activities" happening around the camps—questionable sexual behavior, smuggled booze, and who knows what else. No company can eliminate every infraction, but it was clear the rulebook was collecting dust.

Coming from the corporate world, I knew how fast this could go sideways. Human Resources (HR) policies exist to protect people and organizations. And I made it clear: standard U.S. policies

Chapter 5 A Hot Seat and Some Cold Realities

on relationships and nepotism applied here, too. We might be overseas, but we still represented American values. We needed to live up to them.

One of the worst cases involved a supervisor at a camp who was abusing his position to have "a good time" with third-country national (TCN) female workers mostly from the Philippines. Several TCNs submitted handwritten notes describing encounters in bathrooms, truck sleepers, and other inappropriate locations. Our TTM security team uncovered the notes and brought them to me. The course of action was simple: I terminated him immediately and sent him back to the U.S.

Another case involved a long-tenured KBR Yard Manager in Baghdad along with his two sons, also employed under his supervision. That was nepotism. But it didn't stop there.

Although alcohol was strictly prohibited under general order in Iraq, the rules were much looser at Baghdad Airport and the alcohol found its way to the camps. The sons were caught drinking and partying, which was a hard no. I received reports from our security team, conducted a brief investigation, and terminated both sons for alcohol violations. The father, who was back in the States on vacation, was terminated as well—he'd hired them and allowed the behavior.

He called me afterward. We had a brief, professional conversation. That was the end of it—or so I thought. A few days later, he showed up at my office in Kuwait. I was stunned. How did he get on base? Why would he pay for a flight back just to confront me?

Once I collected myself, I made things very clear. He was no longer a DoD contractor and was not permitted on a U.S. military camp. When he pushed back, I contacted our security team to escort him off the premises, confiscated his badge, and alerted KBR and the military to revoke all access and privileges.

It turned out that KBR hadn't properly collected his badge after termination. That was on them. The man had been making close to $180,000 with a large percentage tax-free, so he wasn't going quietly. He'd paid his own way back, hoping to get back on the gravy train.

And wouldn't you know it—the good ol' boy network came through again. One of his buddies in KBR leadership found him an equivalent job in Afghanistan. Maybe his sons followed him there, too.

Another doozy involved a transportation manager in Kuwait.

Without getting into the weeds, let's just say there were serious issues. After multiple conversations with trustworthy team members and conducting my own investigation, we found enough documented misconduct to terminate him *for cause*.

He had an assistant transportation manager who stayed on but was reassigned to work under British Ray—who wasn't thrilled. She had a questionable reputation, and Ray begged me to reconsider. He didn't want her on his team. But we struck a gentleman's agreement (he is British, after all) and both knew it wouldn't last long. Karma had its own timeline—and it was coming for her, too.

We soon discovered that the transportation manager who had supposedly returned to the U.S. was, in fact, still in Kuwait—now working for an equipment contractor that leased flatbeds to KBR. Surprise, surprise, surprise.

Once we learned where he had landed, I moved to have the contractor removed from KBR's approved vendor list due to clear conflicts of interest. Unfortunately, the process became mired in bureaucracy, and I wasn't successful. Still, one thing was certain: KBR would not be doing business with that individual again.

But not every personnel issue involved misconduct. The most unusual case I dealt with during this period was something else entirely.

A TTM employee at Camp Anaconda, it turned out, was suffering from schizophrenia. And of all the leadership challenges I've faced in my forty-year career, this one remains the most unique.

Chapter 5 A Hot Seat and Some Cold Realities

Hiring 20,000 people in a short time inevitably leads to some hiring missteps. But this one was beyond anything we had anticipated. The incident began when the individual walked into the Army major LNO's office and calmly announced, "I am from Pluto and I'm here to save all Iraqis."

Then he added, "I'm going to give every Iraqi one million dollars."

The major, understandably startled, asked him to repeat himself. The man didn't blink. "I am from Pluto, and I am going to save all Iraqis."

The major quickly contacted the military police (MPs), who arrived and escorted the man to confinement. While in the holding area, he stripped naked, crouched in the corner, and began shaking. When an MP asked what he was doing, he approached—still shaking, still nude—and repeated, "I'm from Pluto. I'm here to save all Iraqis."

Medical personnel were called in, and they were able to restrain and stabilize him. TTM Security submitted a report to me detailing the incident.

Termination wasn't even a question—that was a given. But more importantly, this was clearly a serious medical issue, not a behavioral one. My immediate concern was ensuring the individual received the care he needed and that we could safely return him to the U.S. Within a few days, we were able to stabilize him and arrange for his safe return.

Believe it or not, this wasn't the only schizophrenia-related case we encountered. Another employee, thankfully less dramatic, was also quietly and compassionately returned home. Just footnotes in a chapter of chaos—but reminders of the human toll this operation could take.

Despite all the internal HR issues demanding my time, I also spent considerable energy connecting with both the current Kuwait DPM in Iraq and the newly hired Iraq DPM. As mentioned earlier,

Sand, Grit and Dangerous Supply Missions

the former was still dealing with frustration and resentment, while the latter remained… uniquely difficult to pin down. Meanwhile, I finalized James's appointment as DPM for Kuwait.

As all of these internal dysfunctions were being addressed, the mission itself was becoming more complex—and more dangerous.

By December and January, hostile attacks on convoys were not just increasing—they were escalating.

To put things in perspective, during my tenure, over 700 trucks and trailers were damaged, destroyed, lost, or rendered inoperable. And this was only the beginning.

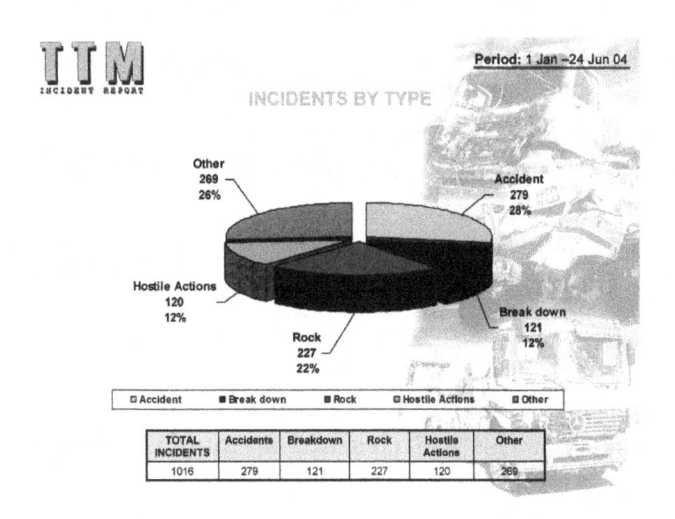

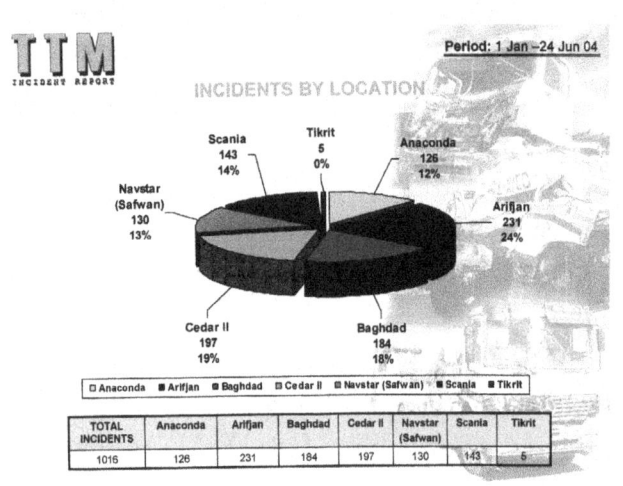

TTM INCIDENT REPORT — INCIDENTS BY TYPE
Period: 1 Jan – 24 Jun 04

- Other: 269 (26%)
- Accident: 279 (28%)
- Break down: 121 (12%)
- Rock: 227 (22%)
- Hostile Actions: 120 (12%)

TOTAL INCIDENTS	Accidents	Breakdown	Rock	Hostile Actions	Other
1016	279	121	227	120	269

TTM INCIDENT REPORT — INCIDENTS BY LOCATION
Period: 1 Jan – 24 Jun 04

- Scania: 143 (14%)
- Tikrit: 5 (0%)
- Anaconda: 126 (12%)
- Navstar (Safwan): 130 (13%)
- Arifjan: 231 (24%)
- Cedar II: 197 (19%)
- Baghdad: 184 (18%)

TOTAL INCIDENTS	Anaconda	Arifjan	Baghdad	Cedar II	Navstar (Safwan)	Scania	Tikrit
1016	126	231	184	197	130	143	5

Chapter 5 A Hot Seat and Some Cold Realities

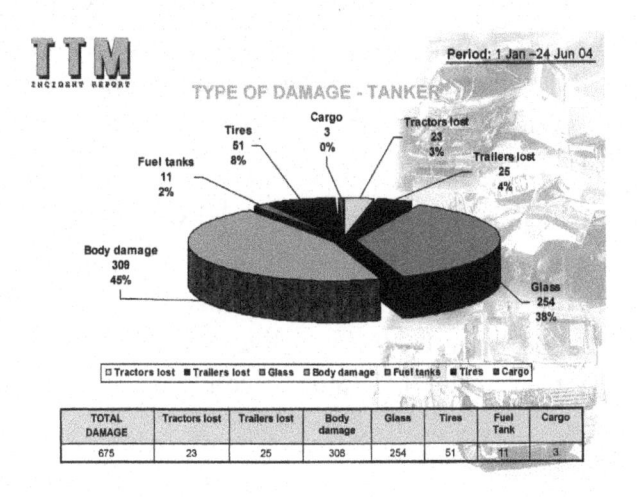

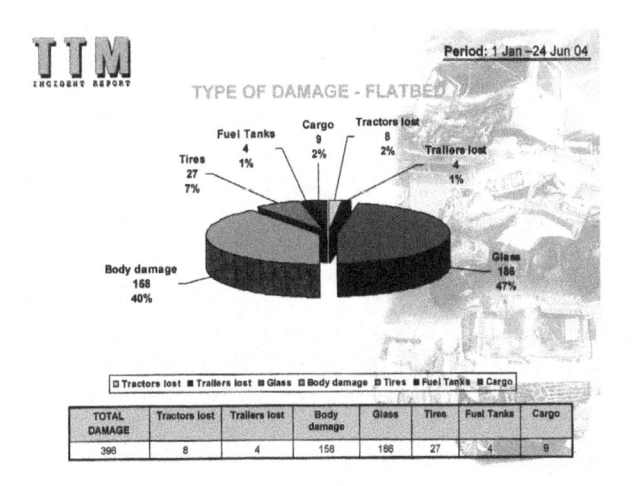

TTM INCIDENT REPORT
Period: 1 Jan – 24 Jun 04
TYPE OF DAMAGE - TANKER

- Tractors lost: 23, 3%
- Trailers lost: 25, 4%
- Glass: 254, 38%
- Body damage: 308, 45%
- Fuel tanks: 11, 2%
- Tires: 51, 8%
- Cargo: 3, 0%

TOTAL DAMAGE	Tractors lost	Trailers lost	Body damage	Glass	Tires	Fuel Tank	Cargo
675	23	25	308	254	51	11	3

TTM INCIDENT REPORT
Period: 1 Jan – 24 Jun 04
TYPE OF DAMAGE - FLATBED

- Tractors lost: 8, 2%
- Trailers lost: 4, 1%
- Glass: 186, 47%
- Body damage: 158, 40%
- Fuel Tanks: 4, 1%
- Tires: 27, 7%
- Cargo: 9, 2%

TOTAL DAMAGE	Tractors lost	Trailers lost	Body damage	Glass	Tires	Fuel Tanks	Cargo
396	8	4	158	186	27	4	9

My first visit to Iraq was eye-opening. It forced me to confront the reality that we were not just supporting a war—we were on the battlefield. Blackhawks hovered overhead. Explosions echoed around camp. Weapons fire, sirens, and ever-present questions about the nearest bunker were part of daily life. This was no post-conflict reconstruction. The war was still on, and the warning signs were everywhere.

As a civilian leader, I had expected challenges—but I was naïve about what exactly they would look like on the ground.

The conflicts between insurgents and U.S. forces were escalating across Iraq. Our convoys traveled along the Main Supply Routes (MSRs), which stretched from Kuwait into Iraq and connected the major military camps. These routes were becoming increasingly dangerous.

The **Sunni Triangle**—a region northwest of Baghdad—was the epicenter of hostility. Bounded by cities like Baghdad, Ramadi, Mosul, and Tikrit, it was home to many of Saddam Hussein's closest loyalists. Other flashpoints like Samarra, Balad, Hit, and Fallujah were part of the Triangle as well.

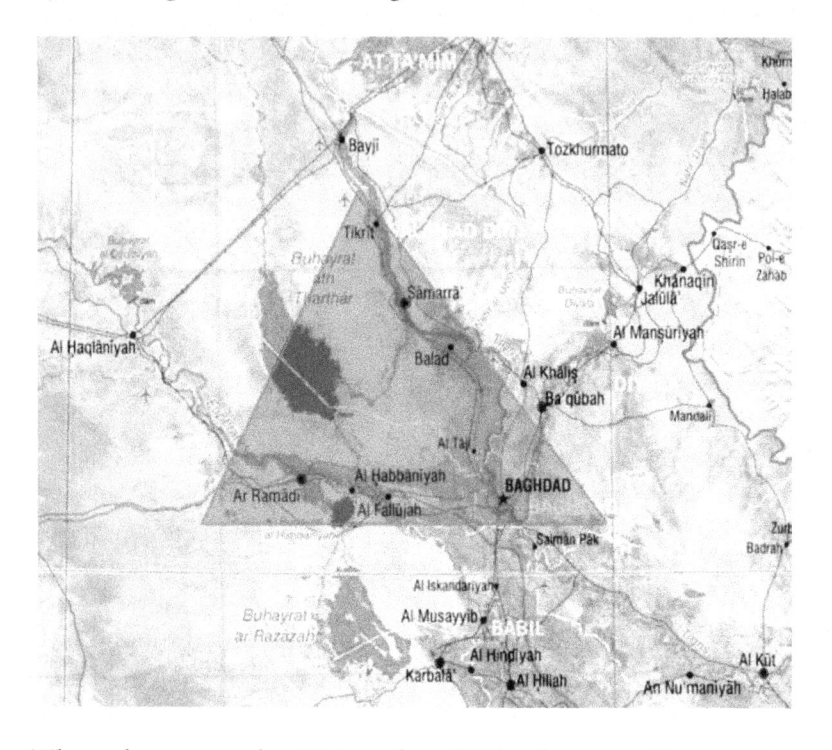

Then there was the **Triangle of Death**, a smaller zone south of Baghdad between the capital and Al Hillah. It became a notorious death trap for Shiite Muslims, civilian contractors, and Iraqi security forces. Al Hillah turned into a launch point for attacks into Baghdad.

Chapter 5 A Hot Seat and Some Cold Realities

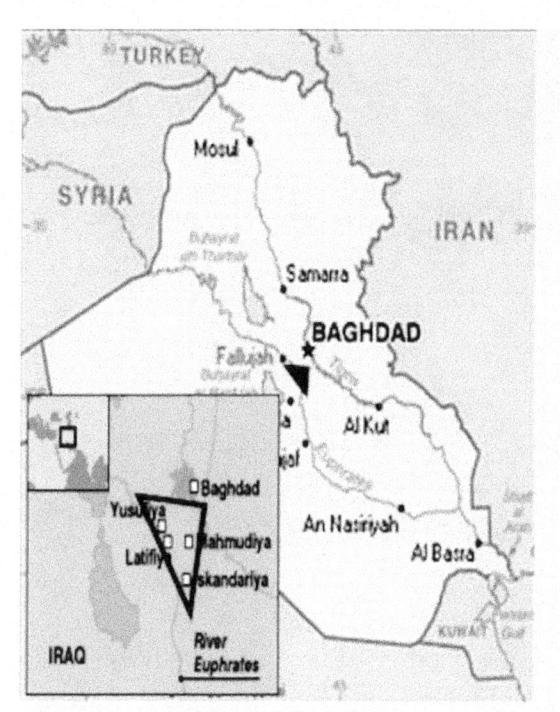

The "Triangle of Death" (U.S. Army/ Center for the Army Profession and Leadership)

And of course, there was Fallujah.

As the transition to Iraq loomed larger and the dangers became more visible, my thoughts often returned to Lana. I felt increasingly torn. Telling her the truth would cause her worry—and would raise questions about why I was even being sent to Iraq in the first place. That certainly hadn't been part of our original understanding.

But staying silent had its risks, too. News coverage might eventually tip her off to what was really happening. There wasn't a clear answer. So I did what I'd already been doing: flipped the internal channel and put it out of my mind. I had too many problems to solve to dwell on what I couldn't change.

CHAPTER 6

THE ANACONDA CORKSCREW

I felt like a seasoned theater travel veteran after my one trip to Anaconda back in November. Hurry up and wait, cargo nets, and the infamous spiral "corkscrew" landing—I'd seen it all. This time, the airfield visit at Arifjan was a bit less eventful. I only had to wait about four hours for a flight.

Seating and accommodations in the Frankfort airport were rough—but nothing compared to what you find on a military base in the Middle East. That brought its own set of challenges. No food, limited seating, and barely any basic supplies. Fortunately, I was now an experienced military traveler. I came prepared with MREs, bottled water, and a few snacks from the Arifjan commissary packed in my backpack. The MREs were my last resort, though I'll admit, some weren't half bad. The desserts, in particular, were surprisingly decent.

Over the past few months, I'd learned that the KBR Movement Control team that reported to TTM and was responsible for scheduling and prioritizing personnel for flights. Because of that, they wanted to "bump" others and get me out sooner. While I understood the importance of reaching Anaconda, I also knew the value of servant leadership. I wanted to send a clear message to the team: they were just as important as I was. So I sat and waited along with everyone else. Once again, the military mantra "hurry up and wait" was in full effect.

When we finally boarded the C-130, it was back to cargo nets. Let me explain what kind of ride that delivers. The image below, from the National Archive, shows some Congressmen in camo en route to Somalia on a C-130 courtesy of the 463rd Tactical Airlift Wing out of Texas. Those cargo nets? They're made for gear, not people. Comfort isn't part of the deal.

The plane carried a handful of contractors and some very young soldiers—barely older than my own boys. What made this flight different was the presence of three female soldiers. I remember them vividly. One looked composed and unshaken. Another seemed anxious and concerned. The third cried the entire flight.

To be honest, I'm still uncomfortable with women being sent into harm's way on the battlefield. I was raised in the South to respect and protect women. The idea of them fighting in war clashes with everything I was taught. It's not sexism—they looked competent, and I wouldn't want to test their mettle—but it was

Chapter 6 The Anaconda Corkscrew

a mindset I struggled with. I didn't know their specific roles, but judging by their demeanors, I assumed they'd be heading to the front lines soon.

While these soldiers were young, many deployed throughout the Middle East were reservists—typically a little older. They joined to serve their country, not necessarily expecting to find themselves on a battlefield halfway across the world. Some had previously been working desk jobs or flipping burgers, and now they were heading into live combat zones. The gravity of that reality was starting to sink in. I looked around and could tell that most of the passengers had never experienced the "Anaconda Joy Ride" before. The silence was thick. I empathized, but I couldn't help the slight grin that formed—I knew what was coming.

Sure enough, as we neared Anaconda, it was time for the spiral descent—and the inevitable wave of mass vomiting that followed. Even as a corkscrew landing veteran, I was still shaking in my boots. Being a stunt pilot was never on my career plan. Honestly, had anyone even designed the C-130 for this kind of flying? At least this time we didn't have to deploy flares from the side gunner's window. He still stared intently at the ground rising up to meet us, but no action this round. We landed safe and sound.

Aside from anticipating the ride, I spent most of the flight thinking, *here we go again*. Another 60 to 90 days of new roles, responsibilities, and operational controls. My mission was to assess the staff, build relationships with military leaders, and gain a thorough understanding of the Anaconda operation so we could effectively fulfill our role. Though TTM was one organization, every camp had its own unique mission, culture, and hierarchy. I knew another period of transition lay ahead—including figuring out who I could trust, much like the "Three Amigos" I had in Kuwait.

I'd heard rumors that the staff had already received the scoop on me. "Fair, open, honest, no-nonsense, straightforward"—that was the word on the street. Not bad. Even in the Middle East, news traveled fast. I'd learned early in my career, thanks to a great mentor, that respect starts with discipline and control—and then comes camaraderie.

As I disembarked the C-130, a couple of staff members were waiting for me—the same ones I'd met during my first trip. One of them was Italo, the Transportation Operations Center (TOC) Manager. I pegged him to be in his mid-thirties—confident, articulate, and with a solid grasp on the business. A strong first impression, and I hoped it would set the tone for things to come. We had a great conversation on the way to the TTM office, where I braced myself for another cramped, barely livable trailer setup.

To my surprise, things had changed.

The first trip was all cots, cold showers, and Third World conditions. But this time, the TTM area had transformed into a large trailer complex. It had several private offices, a driver break room, a full TOC, a room with phones for staff to call home, and even my own private office with sleeping quarters and a shower. I'd learned that when there's strong need, commitment, and of course, funding—things can change fast. Compared to my previous visit, this was practically a resort.

The Iraq DPM met me at the office—not at the airfield, but he and Italo helped with my bags. Italo took charge and gave me a tour of the space. It was becoming more obvious that there were concerns about the DPM. He came off awkward, uncertain, and jittery. I kept wondering, *how did he end up in this role?* But as I reflected on KBR's challenges filling my previous position, it made sense. He had held a leadership role on a previous LOGCAP contract, and when they needed someone fast, he fit the bill. Not that they were looking for a warm body—but they were looking quickly.

The rest of that first day was spent settling in and meeting the leadership team. I met the LNO, a retired Army captain and recent hire. I also connected with members of the TTM leadership: the maintenance manager, the medical staff, the safety and security managers, and both the flatbed and bulk transportation managers.

Chapter 6 The Anaconda Corkscrew

Everyone knew about the termination of the transportation manager in Kuwait. Their body language gave it away—respect, yes, but also uncertainty. Some avoided me entirely.

Still, aside from the DPM, I was initially impressed by the staff. The operation seemed fairly organized. Then again, you can't judge a book by its cover. I knew there was more to uncover, and first impressions are often only the beginning.

As with Kuwait, I conducted one-on-one meetings with the leadership staff to assess their competencies, business acumen, and character, as well as to get their impressions of the operation and the challenges ahead. The LNO was quite candid in her evaluation of the DPM—outspoken, in fact—and shared a variety of concerns about him and the way things had been operating. I quickly concluded she was likely angling for the DPM role herself. My assessment of her was positive overall, though not without reservations. I appreciated her candor and clarity, but I wasn't convinced she was the solution.

Both Transportation Managers seemed competent and knowledgeable about the operation and their respective roles. The Flatbed Manager told me he was glad I'd terminated the Transportation Manager in Kuwait, confirming my impression: "He thought he was in charge." The Bulk Manager was also sharp and would later transition to Kuwait to oversee the entire bulk operation.

In one of those "small world" moments, years later in 2011—long after Iraq and Kuwait—I ran into the same Bulk Transportation Manager again. By then, he was a field manager for Shell Oil, one of our clients at Ryder. I heard his name on a call, asked someone for his full background, and when they confirmed he had worked in Iraq, I gave him a ring. "Are you the Mike from Iraq?" I asked. He replied, "Yeah, Keith. It's me." We had a great conversation reminiscing about our adventures in the Middle East.

The security organization had its own challenges and bureaucratic oddities. Nearly all personnel were retired military—some from special forces. The Security Manager in Kuwait, Joe Brown, was a former police officer. The Anaconda Security Manager, Ray Simpson, a retired Army Ranger, reported to Joe Brown. (Yes, there were a lot of "Rays.") While Ray was respectful, he clearly wasn't thrilled about reporting to someone based in Kuwait. It struck me as odd too, but I had enough on my plate, so I let it ride for the time being. Steve Pulley, another Security Manager, also worked in Anaconda and reported to Ray Simpson.

The TTM security team was unique in that it reported into TTM's leadership hierarchy, whereas all other security departments reported into KBR's LOGCAP III senior leadership chain. This created issues. The security team saw themselves as equal to—or above—military intelligence. One of the recurring problems was clarifying their actual role in security operations. They seemed to think it *was* military intelligence. But we were civilians in a peacetime support operation—at least, in theory.

As insurgent activity ramped up across Iraq, however, the situation became more complex. The resulting tension between the security team and TTM leadership created a contentious, combative atmosphere. It was a classic case of too many chiefs and not enough Indians. Still, after meeting with the leadership staff, I was pleasantly surprised. We had the makings of a solid team.

On a more personal level, day-to-day life came with its own share of challenges and "excitement." Let's start with the bed. The mattress was about as comfortable as the Lufthansa airplane seats—looked like a bed, felt like concrete. That said, I did have a private shower... though the water pressure was a trickle and lukewarm at best—and even that was intermittent. Oh well. As I told the drivers in our all-hands meetings, "We're not in the U.S., and this ain't a Marriott." I tried to stay grateful for the little I had, knowing that many others—especially military personnel—had far less.

Some drivers understood and just sucked it up. Others preferred to vent. Drivers are drivers—and sometimes, complaining is the only shared language you've got in a place like this. With

Chapter 6 The Anaconda Corkscrew

over 20 years in the industry, leading union and non-union drivers alike, I understood the personalities. These were strong-willed people with opinions and real passion—people who, when motivated, could accomplish the extraordinary.

Excitement and risk were amplified by the location of TTM's office complex. It sat roughly 50 yards from the perimeter fence and 100 yards from the fuel bag farms—those massive, flexible bladders storing thousands of gallons of JP8. My office and sleeping quarters were not exactly prime real estate. We were in a high-risk zone, a prime target for insurgents launching RPGs and mortars. After all, what better to aim at than a fuel farm? If one of those had been hit, it would've been spectacular—in the worst way.

One mortar round did land alarmingly close to my quarters at one point. Luckily, no real damage was done. I tried not to dwell on the image of thousands of gallons of JP8 erupting in flames.

Speaking of the perimeter, it marked the line between us and a growingly hostile world. During early tours of Anaconda, I rode around the perimeter road, guarded by watchtowers manned by soldiers ready to respond to threats. I noticed one area just beyond the perimeter with unusually high grass and what appeared to be Iraqis "farming" using hoes and other small tools. Maybe I'm just suspicious by nature, but my first thought was, *What the hell are non-vetted Iraqis doing that close to the perimeter?* The soil didn't look fertile, and something felt off.

I voiced my concerns to military contacts. Not long after, the high grass was cleared and the "farming" ceased. I later heard there had indeed been signs insurgents were using that area as cover to fire at us. I like to think my observation helped prevent future attacks.

But mowing grass wasn't the only line of defense. We had Humvees equipped with .50-caliber machine guns and tracer ammo. From our location near the perimeter, we often saw those Humvees positioned just outside the office complex, returning fire or laying down suppression. If we weren't already in the bunkers, we heard it. That sound still echoes in my ears: *Doo doo doo. Doo doo doo.* A harsh, rhythmic percussion that usually started in the evening and went on for hours. I remember thinking, *please, just hit whatever you're shooting at.* But I suspect many times they were just firing toward likely targets—hoping to discourage insurgents from getting any closer. Sleep? Between the concrete mattress, sirens, and gunfire? Not a chance. *Doo doo doo* was no lullaby.

In fact, that was the soundtrack of my first few weeks at Anaconda. The soldiers had coined a fitting nickname: *Mortarville.* If booze had been allowed, someone would've surely invented a "Mortarrita" to help us forget where we were.

Sirens went off nearly every night, warning of incoming fire. That meant suiting up in full personal protective equipment known as PPE—helmet and a heavy blue flak vest with thick 1' x 1' metal plates in the front and back. They were cumbersome and far from comfortable, but in the early days of LOGCAP III, it was the best we had. We'd rush to the bunkers—buried shipping containers outfitted with wooden benches. Not ideal, but far better than tin huts or tents. And when the sirens kept wailing, we stayed underground.

When you are bone-tired, even the threat of a mortar attack can lose its urgency. But we followed protocol, mostly.

Unlike Kuwait, there were no offsite locations to escape to, no places to break the monotony. Anaconda was a battlefield—a far cry from the "rebuilding Iraq" mission we'd been sold. We were there to support the military and their infrastructure, plain and simple.

If there was one hidden benefit, it came from the daily burden of PPE. Hauling all that weight was its own form of exercise. I maintained my workout routine and stuck to my high-protein, low-carb diet. Italo and I became close—we worked out together, and the gym became our therapy. He was into weightlifting too,

Chapter 6 The Anaconda Corkscrew

and he was strong. Very strong. He benched 350–375 pounds. I hit a personal best of 250—not in his league, but respectable.

From what I observed, Italo had the qualities of a future DPM or PM. After my time in Iraq, I learned he had, in fact, been promoted to PM. Well deserved. I haven't had a better personal trainer since.

Just as it was important to build relationships with TTM staff, it was crucial to identify military leaders I could trust—people who understood the challenges civilians faced in this environment. That wasn't always easy. Soldiers were losing comrades regularly, and it was understandably hard for them to feel much sympathy for civilians who had the option to walk away.

Fortunately, I found two Army officers I came to respect and rely on. They understood we hadn't signed up for combat—and they respected that we were still there, doing our part.

One was Lt. Colonel Sue Davidson, head of Movement Control Command in Iraq. She was confident, empathetic, and a natural leader. I quickly recognized her as a trustworthy ally. As of 2025, she's a Major General—and I can say with confidence, I saw that coming. She and I established regular meetings to coordinate movement plans and share challenges from both sides of the operation.

The second officer came as a complete surprise. I was in a meeting with several military leaders when I glanced over and noticed the rank insignia on the uniform next to me. I looked up—then down at the name tag—and blurted, "Hi, Major ANDREWS!" He looked up, stunned, and said, "Keith?"

It was Chris Andrews. We'd worked together years earlier at Sea-Land in Dallas and had been close friends before losing touch in the late '90s. He was an Army reservist, and I'd heard he'd gone back on active duty—but never imagined we'd reunite in Iraq of all places.

We stepped outside and spent several minutes catching up, trying to wrap our heads around the coincidence. As it turned out, Chris reported up through Sue Davidson's chain of command. We agreed to meet regularly—usually for breakfast two or three times a week—and quickly resumed the close working relationship we'd once had.

While Italo wasn't technically the DPM, he became my de facto second-in-command. Meanwhile, the actual DPM kept his distance. He avoided meetings, was absent more often than not, and when we did meet, it was awkward. I knew something was off, but I didn't have the bandwidth to address it—yet.

My priority was to implement structure, establish control, and set clear expectations—just as I had in Kuwait. I told the leadership team to bring concerns or recommendations directly to me. The DPM realized I was bypassing him and eventually asked why he wasn't being included. My response was blunt: "We need to get shit done, and I don't have time to drag you along." He knew his time was short.

One advantage at Anaconda was the TTM organizational structure—it mirrored what we'd built in Kuwait: DPM, LNO, procurement, security, medical, maintenance, intra-camp buses, water teams, TOC, fuel, and flatbed operations. I quickly mapped out the structure, defined roles, and communicated a clear chain of command—complete with an organizational chart. The clarity was welcomed. Like the military, order and control were essential.

Most of the team got on board quickly. Anaconda, like Kuwait, was now on its way to becoming a well-structured, well-run operation.

Of course, Iraq as a whole was a different story. We were the hub, but the spokes were thin and vulnerable, as we would soon learn all too clearly.

CHAPTER 7

HEARTS, MINDS AND IEDS IN IRAQ

Even in the best of times, trucking in the Middle East was nothing like back in the U.S., where the worst problems were careless drivers, bad weather, or traffic jams. In Iraq, services were scarce, and as the insurgency intensified, trucks began moving exclusively in tight convoys. And no, not the convoys from that 1970s Country and Western song or the movie of the same name. These convoys weren't about freedom or rebellion—they were about survival. The soundtrack wasn't strumming guitars; it was the occasional zip of incoming bullets.

Unlike convoys from Kuwait to Camp Cedar, which were usually flanked by a pair of Army escort vehicles—one at the front and one at the rear of a mile-and-a-half-long line of trucks—many civilian convoys out of Anaconda and northern Iraq had multiple military escorts. In some cases, soldiers even rode shotgun in the cabs alongside the civilian drivers. I believe this was the first time in modern U.S. history that civilians were embedded so directly into a battlefield operation, functioning almost as an extension of the military itself.

Some of the concerns I had from the start of my KBR career were now playing out in full view. Given the increasingly dangerous circumstances, daily coordination with military leadership became essential. TTM convoys were now frequently under attack—from small arms fire, RPGs, mortars, and IEDs. These attacks had already led to hundreds of damaged or lost tractors and trailers, injuries, and tragically, a fatality.

As the insurgency escalated rapidly, we required enhanced collaboration with the military, particularly regarding increased force protection for our civilian convoys. The Army used a five-level force protection system to define threat levels in a hostile environment: Normal, Alpha, Bravo, Charlie, and Delta.

- Normal: A general global threat exists, but routine security measures suffice.
- Alpha: An increased general threat is present, but it remains unpredictable.
- Bravo: A more predictable and elevated threat of terrorist activity exists.
- Charlie: An incident has occurred, or intelligence suggests an attack is likely.
- Delta: An attack has either just occurred or intelligence indicates an attack is imminent at a specific location.

These terms became part of our daily vocabulary, particularly among KBR staff with military backgrounds. Color-coded threat levels were also used, on maps and in tactical communication to quickly convey mission-critical information, adding another layer of terminology.

- Green: Supports current mission without adjustments that can increase time and cost.
- Amber: Minimal or moderate adjustments that can increase time and cost required to accomplish mission.

Chapter 7 Hearts, Minds and IEDs in Iraq

- Red: Cannot fully support current mission or may require significant adjustments that can increase time and cost to accomplish mission.
- Black: Cannot support mission.

The Army's readiness rating system is commonly associated with the BRAG scheme (Black, Red, Amber, Green). Program elements are measured to ensure efficient, effective performance relative to allocated resources. It is critical to report accurate data that provides valuable insight into the "pain points" that need additional support.

Color Ratings	
Color	**Rating Description**
Green:	Supports current mission without work-arounds (adjustments that can increase time and/or cost)
Amber:	Minimal or moderate work-arounds (adjustments that can increase time and/or cost) required to accomplish mission
Red:	Cannot fully support current mission, or may require significant work-arounds (adjustments that can increase time and/or cost) to accomplish mission
Black	Cannot support mission

From my perspective, anything above "green" was cause for serious concern. My mindset was simple: this was no longer "normal," and it was up to the military to determine where we stood—Alpha, Bravo, Charlie, or Delta. I had initially assumed that the losses and attacks were temporary—that we'd eventually bring enough military force to bear to make them stop. I still wanted to support our uniformed colleagues and trusted they would support us in return.

Our civilian convoys were now embedded with military vehicles, but our own trucks—Volvos and Mercedes—weren't armored. And that was a growing problem. Truck doors offer zero protection against bullets, let alone RPGs and IEDs. Drivers voiced their concerns constantly, and I kept pressing both KBR leadership and the military for solutions.

Many drivers started wedging their flak vest plates into their cab doors as makeshift armor. TTM maintenance teams got creative, too—using sheet metal to fashion rudimentary armor. After several months, we finally procured better materials and were able to retrofit some of the trucks. But even that armor offered more psychological comfort than real protection. Given the logistical hurdles of distributing materials across Iraq, installing even basic armor took far longer than it should have.

But it wasn't just enemy fire we were up against. The roads—or lack thereof—posed their own set of challenges. From Camp Cedar north, the Main Supply Routes (MSRs) were often little more than dirt and sand trails, creating blinding dust clouds. Our safety protocol called for trucks to maintain visual contact with the vehicle ahead while keeping a safe distance. It was a buddy system—but in these conditions, that system was almost impossible to maintain.

The result? Rear-end collisions. As noted in the earlier chart, there were 279 accidents most of which were rear-end collisions. In the worst cases, drivers made physical contact before they could even see the truck in front of them. Staying on the road was tough enough, and the constant dust only compounded the danger. Drivers were dealing with basic operational challenges while also bracing for insurgent attacks. I'm sure many of them silently vowed never to complain about traffic back home again.

And we weren't just dealing with bullets or improvised explosive devices (IEDs). Petty theft was rampant. Drivers from other contractors frequently stole tires and parts from our trucks. KBR's fleet was the newest and best equipped in theater, and opportunistic drivers—especially some Turkish contractors staged in Anaconda—were always on the lookout for upgrades. Navistar, Camp Cedar… the thefts happened all over. As usual in war zones, a black market emerged and proved nearly impossible to stamp out.

Rocks thrown by teenage boys were also a daily occurrence. The Iraqis figured out that teenagers could get into the fight

Chapter 7 Hearts, Minds and IEDs in Iraq

without real weapons and without the threat of retaliation from the military. As shown in the earlier charts, there were 279 rock incidents documented that caused 254 glass breakages and other body damage. The convoys were in a world of chaos every day.

TTM and base security did what they could to patrol the staging areas and limit theft, but the problem persisted. It created a constant drain on our parts and supply chains, just one more element to manage in an already chaotic and high-risk operation. Procurement, maintenance, yard management, safety, inventory—everything we did was teetering on the edge of crisis, no matter how much structure we tried to impose. In the midst of all this, I got a new boss.

With my role came significant responsibility, including frequent meetings with senior military officials in Baghdad. Around February or March—exact date's fuzzy—KBR hired retired Brigadier General Craig Peterson to oversee LOGCAP III across Kuwait and Iraq. Unlike his predecessor, John Downey, Craig was based in Baghdad, and I now reported directly to him. This was another KBR attempt to boost credibility with the military.

Craig and I were both passionate leaders. We shared a commitment to the mission but sometimes clashed on how best to achieve it. We had different ideas about our respective roles and about what responsibilities should fall under TTM. Our differing visions complicated matters, but to his credit, Craig was competent—and he knew how to navigate the military chain of command in the region. What added to the complexity was that meetings in Baghdad were no walk in the park.

Anaconda was about 40 miles north of Baghdad, and yes—those trips were by road. In the U.S., a 40-mile drive is nothing—maybe an hour at the most. Seatbelt on, music playing, coffee in hand. Not here. While trips from Kuwait to Camp Cedar were relatively safe and often shared with TTM drivers, travel through central Iraq was a whole different ballgame.

We traveled in armored black Chevy Suburbans, easy to spot with their long antennas and reinforced bumpers. Security details were always on speed dial. And the drivers? They were from Blackwater Security.

Much has been written about Blackwater. The most infamous incident came later, on September 16, 2007, when Blackwater contractors killed seventeen Iraqi civilians in Nisour Square. Their license to operate in Iraq was revoked the next day. But at the time, they were still viewed as elite operators—tough, disciplined, and supposedly there to protect us from the bad guys.

Traveling in armored vehicles through volatile territory, flanked by men with assault rifles and mirrored sunglasses, was both reassuring and unnerving. We weren't just managing logistics—we were living and working on the edge of a warzone.

Our first trip from Anaconda to Baghdad was, to put it mildly, eventful. From what I recall, the 40-mile journey took about two hours—two hours filled with tense moments and surreal scenes that were, at best, nerve-wracking.

Our Blackwater escorts on this trip were former Iraqi pilots. Yes, Iraqi pilots—men who once held elite status in Saddam Hussein's regime were now working as high-priced security contractors. Given the state of Iraqi society at the time, I suppose they were grateful for the decent-paying work, but I doubted they had much enthusiasm for the job.

They had plenty of latitude in how they did their job, and even more attitude. Their mission was singular: get their passengers from Point A to Point B as fast as possible and without incident. That meant no stopping. None. Slowing down or stopping was an invitation to ambush. Along the way, we passed through numerous small towns—none of them looked prosperous, and all of them looked hostile. It was the stereotypical image of a Third World country, but what really stuck with me were the eyes of the locals—eyes filled with wariness, despair, and, often, open hatred.

Chapter 7 Hearts, Minds and IEDs in Iraq

Our black Suburban, with its long antennas, stood out like a sore thumb. We weren't just noticeable; we were a symbol of everything they'd come to resent. At times, we had to slow down to avoid people, livestock, or chaotic traffic. That's when the escorts would go into action—bumping civilian vehicles off the road, brandishing their AKs out the windows to make a path. I thought to myself, *this is some real shit*. At one point, we passed so close to Iraqi children that I could see their eyes. Unlike most American kids, their eyes weren't filled with wonder—they were full of anger and hopelessness. It was heartbreaking. I remember thinking, *there has to be a better way*. But that was far beyond my scope. All I could do was try to make sure we got our part right and didn't make things worse.

The Blackwater team's "don't stop for anything" policy was put to the test mid-journey. At one point, the MSR was blocked—never a good sign. Without hesitation, our escorts veered off the road and into a field of high grass. We were bouncing around like we were on a carnival ride. When we attempted to rejoin the MSR, the armored SUV—loaded down with six big passengers—got stuck on an asphalt berm. So there we were: in the Sunni Triangle, in a conspicuous black Suburban, stuck on the side of the road. Not a friendly face in sight.

The escorts jumped out with weapons at the ready. I couldn't help but laugh in disbelief. *Seriously? After everything else, now this?* Fortunately, a military Humvee with a U.S. soldier team arrived about 10 minutes later and pulled us free. Another surreal experience in what was beginning to feel like a long string of them. We made it to Baghdad in one piece, and I did my best to wear my "all in a day's work" expression.

The visit included meetings with Craig and other LOGCAP III senior leaders, as well as high-ranking military officials and our TTM staff. We also toured the Green Zone—the Coalition Provisional Authority's headquarters until June 2004, when the Iraqi Interim Government took over. TTM had about 100 employees in Baghdad handling yard operations, postal services, and potable water transport.

But the TTM team in Baghdad was something of an afterthought, caught in a tug-of-war between leadership and operations. Conditions for staff there lagged far behind those in Anaconda and other locations. That led to many uncomfortable conversations with KBR's camp leadership—because our people deserved to be treated with the same seriousness and respect.

One of the more surreal aspects of the visit was touring two of Saddam's palaces. Yes—actual palaces, filled with gold and luxurious amenities. The U.S. had taken them over and turned them into offices, which felt strange but also necessary. We needed operational space, and this was available.

James and the Anaconda DPM joined me for a meeting with senior military officers, where we were scheduled to present an overview of the TTM operation. James went first—his presentation was solid: clear, concise, informative. The Anaconda DPM followed... and it was a trainwreck. He could barely complete a sentence and stumbled through the entire thing. I was seated next to James and "Houston Ray," and I wanted to crawl under the table.

It was obvious our credibility was slipping fast. So as soon as the DPM finished, I stood up, introduced myself, and took over the room. My goal was simple: convey confidence and make it clear that *he* didn't represent *us*. I did my best to reset the tone, and in the end, the military leaders seemed receptive. Still, I got some honest feedback afterward about the DPM—and it was clear: something needed to change, and soon.

That meeting also revealed a key insight into James' personality. Midway through, a brigadier general walked in—someone who had served with James in the past. All the military personnel stood and saluted. Not knowing the exact protocol, I stood too. James, however, stayed seated. I whispered, "What are you doing?" He replied calmly, "We're not in the Army."

After the general spoke briefly—receiving applause and praise from the military audience—James stood up and said something like, "TTM isn't the military. We're here to support the military, and we expect them to support us. While you salute the General, you also need to understand *our* role."

I nearly choked. *Oh shit*, I thought. But the general smiled and nodded. He clearly respected James' direct, honest approach. As had I come to. James had a reputation, and it seemed to work in his favor.

The trip back to Anaconda had its share of drama too. As we passed through Taji, our convoy was slowed by civilian vehicles and buses. Our escorts made it very clear that we had priority—honking, maneuvering aggressively, even bumping a bus and waving rifles out the window. Winning hearts and minds, we were not.

Approximately five miles later, the MSR was blocked again. This time, there was no grassy detour. Our escorts swerved to the front of the halted traffic and discovered the cause—an IED. If you've seen *The Hurt Locker*, you've got a sense of what happened next.

We were about fifty yards away as the Explosive Ordinance Disposal Unit (EOD) unit responded. A soldier in a bomb suit walked out and placed another device near the IED. A few minutes later—boom. The blast flash, sound, and shockwave hit all at once. Fifty yards suddenly didn't feel very far.

It was a *"shit in my pants"* moment, and everyone in the vehicle laughed as I jumped in my seat. "Keith, you, okay?" someone asked. I replied, "F... no!" Eventually, we were cleared to continue, and we made it back to Anaconda—me with a new respect for just how thin the line between "safe" and "not" really was.

Back at Anaconda, tensions were rising. The insurgency was growing across northern Iraq, and I was becoming increasingly frustrated with the level—or lack—of force protection for our convoys. I visited the staging areas daily to speak with the drivers. Some were determined to tough it out. Others were clearly shaken and wanted to be relocated either to Kuwait or Camp Cedar.

I empathized. These were not the circumstances we thought we were signing up for. I reminded them that while the situation had changed, we all had signed on the dotted line. They had two choices: remain in their current roles or return to the U.S. They'd been hired as drivers based in Iraq, and that reality hadn't changed.

As a partial response to growing concerns, we created a tenured hierarchy—newer drivers were required to work in Iraq before being considered for transfer to Kuwait or intra-camp roles. During in-theater orientation sessions, I painted a clear and realistic picture of the current threat landscape. Some didn't like what they heard and resigned on the spot. Others tried to tough it out but eventually decided to leave. I couldn't blame them.

At the time, I thought I understood. But things were about to escalate in ways none of us—least of all me—could have imagined. I needed a new frame of reference.

I just didn't have one.

CHAPTER 8

CHAOS, FRUSTRATION AND A TARGET ON OUR BACK

After everything I'd experienced in my first few months, my status as a TTM veteran was firmly established. I had seen it all—or so I thought. But what had once seemed anomalous or extreme was quickly becoming routine. The chaos was accelerating, and the meaning of *veteran* was shifting.

By March 2004, concerns and fears within the TTM organization were escalating. Operations and security staff were in constant contact—by email, in person, and across every communication channel available. Our security team was receiving steady streams of information, some confirmed, some speculative, and much of it conflicting with military assessments.

Meetings with the military became increasingly tense. The friction wasn't just between us and the military; it was internal as well. KBR leadership—corporate, theater operations, and security—were all at odds. The environment was frenzied, combative, and relentlessly stressful. No one could agree on the best way to support our staff or our end customers: the soldiers. The bottom line was simple and inescapable. We weren't supposed to be on a battlefield. Yet here we were, in the thick of it.

The military needed our convoys to deliver fuel and supplies to sustain their fight against escalating insurgencies—and we needed their protection to do it. But the feedback loop between need and support was broken, and no real solution was in sight. The stress was relentless—twenty-four hours a day, seven days a week. By late March, violence surged across Iraq. Then came March 31, 2004—a defining moment.

In Fallujah, Iraqi insurgents ambushed a convoy carrying four Blackwater USA contractors working a delivery for food caterer ESS. The men were pulled from their vehicles, beaten, and set on fire. Their mutilated bodies were hung from a bridge for the world to see. It was a gruesome, unmistakable wake-up call. For us civilians, the message couldn't have been clearer: you are no longer on the sidelines.

The military was battling both Sunni and Shiite uprisings across the Sunni Triangle, and as mentioned, what was grimly known as the *Triangle of Death*. April 2004 would go down as one of the deadliest months of the war—for soldiers and contractors alike. And TTM was right in the middle of it all, entangled in the chaos.

As things escalated, I became increasingly difficult to be around. My no-nonsense approach had always been firm, but now it was fused with frustration, stress, and anger. I was constantly on edge, worn thin by the endless debates, endless threats, and the complete disconnect between our civilian role and the reality we were facing.

We were not supposed to be in a war. The war, they said, was "over." But no one told that to the Iraqis still firing RPGs, planting IEDs, or launching mortar attacks. Apparently, the word "war" no longer applied to actual battles, bloodshed, or daily combat. At best, military leadership labeled it an "insurgency." But that word

Chapter 8 Chaos, Frustration and a Target on Our Back

didn't begin to capture the scale or intensity of what was unfolding around us.

To put it in perspective, battles were raging throughout the Sunni Triangle. Fallujah became the epicenter of fierce resistance. Though U.S. forces wouldn't fully retake the city until months later—during the "second" Battle of Fallujah in November 2004, code-named *Operation Phantom Fury*—it was already a warzone. By year's end, nearly forty percent of Fallujah lay in ruins. Mosques had been converted into weapons caches. Insurgents were deeply embedded, and U.S. troops fought street by street to reclaim the city.

Meanwhile, multiple battles broke out across the Triangle, particularly in March and April 2004. Fighting was erupting on several fronts. KBR had people everywhere—in and around the Triangle, the Triangle of Death, and beyond. TTM supported missions in these hot zones, and every movement was closely monitored by both military command and our operations teams.

Much like the militia at the start of the American Revolution, we still thought of ourselves as civilians. But in reality, we were soldiers in all but name. We operated under a constant threat surrounded by Black Hawks, .50-caliber machine guns, small arms fire, IEDs, RPGs, and mortar rounds. This was not a peacetime DoD support operation. It was a full-blown battlefield. And we were 100 percent dependent on the military for oversight and protection.

Later, when I looked back and researched our situation, I realized just how unique it was. This was the first time in modern U.S. history that civilians had been contracted to directly support a military operation on an active battlefield. We were pioneers—whether we wanted to be or not.

Thankfully, many soldiers and officers recognized we didn't belong in that environment. They did their best to provide cover, support, and guidance. We were grateful—eternally grateful.

To their credit, our security teams worked hard to gather and filter intelligence. They gathered human intel from drivers, civilians, and military contacts. They didn't have all the answers, and they lacked the deep in-country experience that might've connected all the dots—but they were right about a lot of what was happening.

Still, no one fully understood *why* Iraq seemed to explode at that particular time. Later, I came to learn that March was an important month in the Islamic calendar—a time when people gathered, reflected, and, as it turned out, were vulnerable to extremist influence. Insurgents took full advantage of that, stirring up resentment and rallying anger toward American presence and occupation—especially those black Suburbans filled with Blackwater contractors.

March and April became the deadliest months of the war up to that point. Suicide bombings in Baghdad and Karbala killed nearly 200 people at the peak of the Shia festival of Aashurah. In Fallujah, *Operation Vigilant Resolve* kicked off on April 4 in response to the Blackwater contractor killings. U.S. forces sealed off the city and launched a major assault on April 7. But even after three days of brutal fighting, they had only secured about fifteen percent of the city.

At the same time, the Mahdi Army—a powerful Shia militia—seized full control of Kut and partial control of other key cities: Najaf, Karbala, and Kufa. The entire country seemed to be unraveling. You get the picture. All hell was breaking loose.

And there we were—civilians trying to do our jobs while caught in the crossfire. We were discovering, in real time, that bravery and heroism had become unofficial parts of our job descriptions. But we were also discovering something else—something few back home truly understood: the U.S. military could not conduct this war without us.

Chapter 8 Chaos, Frustration and a Target on Our Back

Our brothers and sisters in uniform had the equipment and the training, but they were stretched thin, fighting a highly motivated, well-equipped, and at times suicidal enemy that moved freely among civilians. The battle for Iraq was entering a new phase—one that was going to test all of us, soldier and contractor alike.

April was the month of hell, and I found myself caught squarely between TTM drivers, KBR leadership, security personnel, and military command. I was acutely aware of the mounting violence, the increasing number of ambushes and attacks, and the spiraling casualty counts. The constant back-and-forth between TTM, KBR Security, and KBR senior leadership grew increasingly heated and volatile. Emails were flying. Nerves were frayed. Frustration became the ambient air we breathed.

Why were we here? What were we going to do? Could we really depend on the military to protect us?

My stress level was unlike anything I had ever experienced. I was doing my best to lead a civilian logistics operation in what had become an unacknowledged warzone. It felt like standing on the deck of the Titanic after it hit the iceberg. You knew things were getting worse, but what exactly could you do? There was no clear path forward. We were running on caffeine, adrenaline, and muscle memory. It was only our collective skills, professionalism, and shared commitment that held us together.

As the days blurred, I made a point to regularly meet with drivers and TTM staff. My job was to lead from the front—to project calm, control, and confidence, even when I was running on fumes. Those conversations with the drivers were often the most inspiring part of my day. Many of them remained fiercely committed to the mission, willing to do whatever it took to support the troops.

Despite my own growing concern about the erosion of our civilian status, I shared that sense of duty. If we could just do our part well—keep the wheels turning—maybe we could help hold the line. The Titanic analogy wasn't far off: no one was getting off anytime soon, so we had to do everything we could to stay afloat.

While I was in frustrating meetings with KBR leadership and tense, often unproductive, conversations with military commanders, the TTM team kept doing their job—professional, steady, and unwavering. They knew, as I did, that if we failed, the mission would fail.

A senior Army logistics officer put it plainly: "KBR still delivers eighty to ninety percent of the military's fuel. If KBR doesn't move, neither can the U.S. Army." He reminded me—and I never forgot it—that unlike soldiers, contractors don't take orders. But the food still had to get there. The fuel still had to arrive. And we were the ones delivering it. This was war. And we were up at bat.

I no longer had the luxury of questioning the decisions of the Department of Defense or the U.S. Government. I had a job to do. It was my responsibility to lead TTM through the storm, not analyze how we ended up in it.

On April 2, KBR Security's Rex Williams issued a "Threat Update Document," noting increasingly sophisticated attacks on convoys and predicting a surge in violence over the coming weekend—Good Friday through Easter Sunday. The document included a map and two security calendars. One marked April 9 as the first anniversary of the American occupation of Baghdad—a symbolic flashpoint. The other noted that Easter weekend overlapped with Arbaeen, a major Shia religious observance.

Then on April 4, Ray Simpson emailed me and others, proposing we "hold back on moving convoys" due to escalating threats. He was relaying concerns from Steve Pulley, who had intel suggesting coordinated attacks were forming in Baghdad. Rex Williams reported that attacks in the area for the week ending April 3 had jumped by fifty percent over the prior week.

By April 5, KBR Security pushed to halt all convoy movements. Ray Simpson, under direction from Security Director Joe Brown,

Chapter 8 Chaos, Frustration and a Target on Our Back

issued a stop order. I pushed back immediately. "This is not a decision Joe—or I—can make," I told them. "Only Craig Peterson or Ray Rodon can make this decision."

That same day, Muqtada al-Sadr—a radical Shia cleric—called for jihad against Coalition forces and sought to take control of Al Kut, An Najaf, and Sadr City. The chaos spread like wildfire. Though the Mahdi Army couldn't stand toe-to-toe with U.S. Abrams tanks, they knew the weak point: the supply chain. The tanks needed fuel, and fuel convoys made for easier targets.

By Wednesday, April 7, Security was beyond frustrated. Joe Brown reiterated dire warnings about what April 9 and 10 might bring. That same day, I responded to an email from a friend back home on April 8 who had asked where I was. My reply:

"In a damn war zone. One of my convoys was hit with 14 mortars, 6 RPGs, 5 IEDs, and small arms fire. It was a basic ambush. Amazingly, no one was injured or killed."

That night, April 8, militia forces loyal to al-Sadr destroyed eight bridges and overpasses near Convoy Support Center Scania along MSR Tampa, effectively halting all northbound traffic into Baghdad and the Sunni Triangle. The U.S. military scrambled to construct temporary crossings. Supplies were running thin, and the coalition's fuel-hungry Abrams tanks were already living on borrowed time.

At BIAP (Baghdad International Airport), 2LT James L. McCormick's Humvee gun truck, *Zebra*, came under sustained enemy fire. He and SPC Brandon Lawson were seriously wounded, fighting off the ambush for 20 agonizing minutes. BIAP was a critical logistics node, including for TTM operations like postal and equipment support. Losing it wasn't an option.

April 8 began badly and spiraled fast. The volume of emails, arguments, and heated calls was off the charts. It was total insanity. Chaos had taken hold. I was on constant calls with Craig Peterson, and our conversations weren't exactly collaborative. Once a

General, always a General. But as James had pointed out in Iraq, "TTM is not in the military." That was the crux of it—Craig never quite seemed to understand that.

"Gentlemen... HOT!!! We have a convoy... that is in direct engagement at this time... and pleads for immediate assistance," a security advisor reported early on April 8.

More grim updates followed:

"We are taking on gunfire, mortars, RPGs, small arms fire—you name it, we got hit. We are losing trucks one by one... My driver and I were lucky to get out alive."

I was bombarded—emails from TOCs in Kuwait, from KBR Security leadership, constant comms with the TTM TOC in Anaconda. And in the middle of it, I was trying to keep a civilian supply operation running in a warzone. The military was trying to help, but the reality was that their protection couldn't stretch far or fast enough.

I barely slept over the three-day span from April 7 to 9. When I did try to rest, I asked Italo to wake me after an hour in case of any incidents. Those one-hour naps never materialized. I was lucky if I could close my eyes for a few minutes and reset my brain before the next emergency hit.

We embedded Steve Pulley with the military for real-time updates. I transitioned convoy movement control from the Kuwait TOC to Anaconda to create better cadence and continuity. The Movement Control Manager in Anaconda coordinated directly with my friend, Army Major Chris Andrews. He and I stayed in constant communication.

Despite everything falling apart outside the wire, we kept twice-daily meetings with the TTM leadership team. We checked alignment, expectations, staffing, morale, and most importantly—how were the drivers holding up? I visited the convoy staging areas every morning and talked with them myself. Managers confirmed what I saw firsthand: the team was steady, strong, and determined.

Chapter 8 Chaos, Frustration and a Target on Our Back

I was proud—beyond proud—of their resilience. They kept the operation going when it would've been easier to quit. We had strong military support, we had raised the alarm, and I believed we were getting closer to a turning point. Surely things would improve soon.

We had made it this far. How much worse could it get?

CHAPTER 9

ALL HELL BREAKS LOOSE

By the end of Thursday, April 8th, one TTM driver was dead and more than 120 had been attacked. Several were seriously injured. The security organization feared that sectarian violence could escalate the danger on April 9th. They spoke with one voice, calling for a suspension of convoys. And so began the juggling act—and the circus. The security organizations were not the U.S. military and lacked access to real-time intelligence. The soldiers needed fuel and supplies. The TTM drivers needed leadership and protection. What we needed was better force protection.

"I say we halt them for a day at least and consider it a safety/security stand-down and mental health day," wrote KBR security chief George Seagle on April 8. "There is tons of intel stating tomorrow will be another bad day." George was responsible for all KBR security personnel, except TTM. TTM security reported to TTM—a point of contention—but KBR believed that separation was necessary due to the transportation aspect of the operation. I agreed with George's assessment and sent an email stating, "Another day like today and we will lose most of our drivers." That email would later haunt me in litigation. Many interpreted "lose" to mean fatalities. At the time, I was referring to resignations.

During this period, I frequently reached out to friends and family by phone and email. I needed a sense of normalcy and an outlet to vent, though I couldn't share everything that was going on. I remember a conversation with my brother Leo. He told me, "Don't let them get to you. Do the right thing." That was the issue—what was the right thing? Lana, by then aware I was in Anaconda, and I had emotional conversations. She would plead, "Please get out of there. I love you." I'd reply, "I love you, but I have a job to do, and I can't abandon my team." I was being pushed, pulled, and prodded from every angle.

Despite the ongoing hostility, KBR security advisors lacked the authority to halt convoy deployment. They were advisors—not military. On April 5th, Craig Peterson sent an email making it clear that he and I would work with the military to determine the status of convoy movements. That declaration angered the security team and created tremendous animosity and friction.

"Yeah, well, I've been authorized for a year now to stop convoys," a security manager stated, "and now all of a sudden Keith [Richard] . . . is the only one who can. . . Well partner, believe me, the ball is in his court." I spoke with him to explain the situation because we needed their support, but we also needed one belly button to push. And I was that belly button.

Craig Peterson and I were in constant—sometimes heated—communication about KBR's contractual obligations with the military, which he repeatedly referred to as "the customer." He was adamant that the civilian truckers had to move when the military called for them.

After a meeting with military commanders, Craig wrote in an email that "it was reiterated that only the Army leadership can stop convoys" and that we needed "to team our way into decisions. We cannot unilaterally decide these things on our own." I hesitantly agreed, understanding the broader mission of supporting the troops, but I remained deeply concerned about our drivers.

Chapter 9 All Hell Breaks Loose

There was sharp disagreement inside the company. "We cannot allow the Army to push us to put our people in harm's way," wrote Tom Crum, then KBR's Chief Operating Officer for logistics operations.

"We need to work with the Army, without a doubt, when it comes to stopping convoys. But if we in management believe the Army is asking us to put our KBR employees in danger, which we are not willing to accept, then we will refuse to go," Crum insisted. He and Craig debated constantly. Ultimately, Craig was the LOGCAP leader—the top authority in the chain of command.

I also pushed back. "Our drivers signed up knowing there was some level of hostility," I wrote, "but they didn't expect to be in the middle of a war."

A liaison working for Craig sent me a scolding note: "[Peterson] says that if the client pushes, then we push." The note further stated that convoys should only stop if security was inadequate or the move "doesn't pass the Commonsense Safety Test." I had no patience for this bureaucratic nonsense. "Who in the hell determines adequate security?" I wrote back. "This is a roll of the dice. None of this passes any of those tests if you ask me."

I followed with a hard truth: "With this decision I cannot continue my employment with KBR. I cannot consciously sit back and allow unarmed civilians to get picked apart. Putting civilians in the middle of a war is not in any contract, policy, or procedure. I will not allow this to happen." Houston Ray and John Downey, the previous KBR LOGCAP III leader, both contacted me in support and tried to talk me out of resigning. I explained that this was no longer about leading a supply chain—this was insanity. They urged me to stay and promised their support. In the end, I decided to stay, much to Lana's dismay.

After a long day of armed attacks on TTM drivers and heated arguments with Security, Craig, Ray, and others, I sent an email at 10:26 p.m. on April 8 using a now-familiar phrase: "If the military pushes, we push." This was after many contentious conversations with military leaders, including direct discussions between Craig and in-theater Army command.

Supplies were urgently needed at BIAP. According to an Army report, dwindling fuel supplies threatened to idle two military divisions. Military commanders called for 200,000 gallons of jet fuel to be rushed from Camp Anaconda. The urgency and fluidity of the operation were becoming uncontrollable. The military needed fuel throughout northern Iraq, and TTM was the supplier. At one point, the military considered driving our trucks—but there were two problems. First, military trucks were automatic transmissions; TTM trucks had European-style standard clutches. Most soldiers didn't know how to drive them, and there was no time for training. Second, they didn't have enough troops.

"This has to happen... 1st light has to go... emergency push," read notes from an Army report on April 8, referring to the fuel convoy to BIAP.

Gen. James E. Chambers, head of the Army's 13th Corps Support Command (COSCOM) at Anaconda, issued explicit orders to his officers: "Not moving critical support is not an option," he wrote before dawn on April 9. "We just have to figure out how to mitigate the risks." That statement sent me into a rage. I understood military rules of engagement—but this wasn't about mitigation. Civilian fatalities are not an acceptable risk. What does mitigation even mean in this context? We needed full-scale protection.

The orders were passed down to military escort units with a comment from an Anaconda commander: "Note the statement about convoys. They move."

But even within the military, there was dissent. At a 6 a.m. intelligence briefing on April 9, Chambers was informed that the road to Baghdad's airport was too dangerous for civilians, according to Col. Ray Josey, his operations head. "We should just stand down," Josey said he told Chambers.

Chapter 9 All Hell Breaks Loose

Others disagreed, saying the route was safe enough. In the end, Chambers ordered the jet fuel convoy to move—but added more Humvees, extra ammunition, and an armed soldier in every truck cab. Was that their definition of mitigation? To me, it was madness. Shortly after, Chambers relieved Josey of his post.

At KBR, the decision to move convoys was again in doubt as dawn broke.

At 6:44 a.m. on April 9—almost an hour after Chambers' order—I sent a message to all drivers: "No convoys are to move" between Anaconda and the military bases south of Baghdad, based on the military's own threat level. That stand-down lasted just 25 minutes, overridden by updated threat level information from COSCOM command in Anaconda.

At 7:14 a.m., the TTM TOCs issued another message: "Per Keith Richard, project manager, all traffic is to proceed as normal. All… traffic lanes are open in all directions." The military was now providing real-time threat level updates and had been designated as the sole authority for such assessments. I was directed to rely only on Lt. Col. James Carroll, based in Anaconda, for all decisions on convoy movement and threat levels.

Meanwhile, confusion reigned within Army ranks. On April 9, different military units had conflicting views on the status of the route to BIAP. The Baghdad-based unit monitoring road safety listed the road as a no-go all day, but COSCOM commanders in Anaconda did not consult that unit before dispatching the convoy led by Thomas Hamill. Convoys were tracked using the names of their Convoy Commanders—Hamill was one of them. I was doing everything I could to maintain coordination between the military and convoy operations, but it was an ever-changing, chaotic, and confusing situation.

At KBR Security, however, there was no such confusion. Six KBR convoys had already been attacked near the airport that morning. Stephen Pulley, TTM's security advisor at Camp Anaconda, remained in frequent contact with the road monitoring unit and received repeated assurances that the routes were closed. He and I were in constant communication.

By 10:05 a.m. on April 9, news spread of an attack on Convoy Commander Reedel's group. Joe Daniel reported to me that Reedel was safe at BIAP by 10:00 a.m. Hamill was still staged at Anaconda.

At 10:28 a.m., an email reported that three convoys were under attack near the MSR Tampa/Sword junction outside Baghdad. Twelve minutes later, the military command in Baghdad designated MSR Tampa as "red" status—signifying no civilian travel permitted. At that moment, three convoys—Teddy, Tomaszewski, and Watson—were under active attack in the BIAP area. A fourth convoy, led by Reedel, had passed through the same combat zone only minutes earlier. A fifth, commanded by Larvenz, had been diverted from MSR Sword to BIAP for safety. The situation reports (SITREP) from the TTM TOC in Kuwait included:

1. The Henderson convoy was attacked between Anaconda and BIAP.
2. The Reedel convoy came under attack in the BIAP area.
3. Reedel lost his truck, along with at least six others.
4. At least eight drivers from Reedel's convoy were missing.
5. Multiple drivers were injured in the Reedel attack.
6. Teddy, Watson, and Tomaszewski convoys were actively under fire in the BIAP area.
7. The Larvenz convoy was attacked on Sword and diverted into BIAP for safety.
8. The Daryl Watson convoy was attacked while departing BIAP.
9. The Reed convoy reported heavy fire between Abu Ghraib prison and BIAP.
10. The military had designated MSR Tampa as "red."

Chapter 9 All Hell Breaks Loose

The email from the TTM TOC and actual convoy status report are captured below.

Destination	Mission	Origin	Convoy Commander	SITREP
TQ	HETS	VIRG	SALVADOR	ARRIVED AT WARHORSE RON
TAJI	HETS	CDR2	HAWKINS	AT NAVISTAR
TAJI	HETS	UDARI	MCGORDY	NORTH TO TAJI
ANAC	TANKER	AFJN	TEDDY	TEDDY UNDER MORTAL FIRE. 1 TCN DOWN, 1 SYTEM DOWN, HAMILL HEADED IN THAT DIRCETION. NO CONTACT WITH HAMILL. PANIC BUTTON BEIGN PRESSED... UNCOFRM AT BIAP
BIAP	TANKER	AFJN	TOMASZEWSKI	ENRT TO CDR2
CDR2	TANKER	AFJN	MCKEE	RON AT CDR2
CDR2	TANKER	AFJN	KING	RON AT SCANIA
ANAC	TANKER	AFJN	BRINKLEY	RON CDR2 4/6
CDR2	TANKER	AFJN	HELOU	RON AT CDR2
ANAC	TANKER	AFJN	VEGA	RON CDR2 4/6
CDR2	TANKER	AFJN	SANCHEZ	RON AT CDR2
ANAC	TANKER	AFJN	REEDEL	ANAC SOUTH SCNI 0705/2.8KM SW TAJI/HOSTILE ACTION AT INTERSECTION TAMPA-SWORD LOST ONE ASSET NO REPORTED INJURIES / CONVOY WILL DIVERT TO BIAP FOR SAFETY / ONE SYSTEM LOST / CC REPORTING SEVERAL AIMS SUB-CONT DRIVERS MISSING ALL EXPATS ACCOUNTED FOR ### AT BIAP NOW####
ANAC	TANKER	AFJN	HENDERSON	RON AT BIAP
BIAP	TANKER	AFJN	PHELPS	HOLDING AT SCANI...WILL RON THERE
ANAC	TANKER	AFJN	CHUMAK	HOLDING AT SCANI...WILL RON THERE
BIAP	TANKER	AFJN	UPSON	RON AT BIAP
ANAC	TANKER	AFJN	MILLER	RON SCNI 4/6
ANAC	TANKER	CDR2	FORD,ELLERY	RON ANAC 4/6
ANAC	TANKER	CDR2	WESLEY	RON AT SCANIA
ANAC	TANKER	CDR2	LONGSTREET	RON AT ANAC
SCNI	TANKER	CDR2	FORD,COREY	RON SCNI 4/6
SCNI	TANKER	CDR2	RICE	RON AT SCANIA
ANAC	TANKER	CDR2	GOLEMAN	MISSION COMPLETE
BIAP	TANKER	CDR2	SINGLETON	RON BIAP 4/6
BIAP	TANKER	ANAC	REINA	AT BIAP
BIAP	TANKER	ANAC	HAMILL	TAKING FIRA NEAR TAJI CANT REACH HIM ON QC NO CONTACT WITH THIS CONVOY ??
BIAP	TANKER	ANAC	STONEBREAKER	AT ANAC
B APO	MAIL	KAPO	ALESTOCK	AT BIAP MISSION COMPLETE
ADDER	MAIL	KAPO	WILLIAMS	MISSION COMPLETE
BAPO	MAIL	KAPO	CALDWELL	RON AT SCANIA
ADDER	MAIL	KAPO	TODD	HOLD AT CDR2
TIKR	MAIL	BALAD	MAUST	RON A TIKRIT
	MAIL		WATSON	ENROUTE TO CDR2
TQ	MAIL	BAPO	REED	DEPARTING ABU GHURAYB HEADED TO BIAP
TAJI	MAIL	ANAC	RANDALL	NOT DEPARTED AS OF YET
BIAP	MAIL	KAPO	COBY	ENRT TO CDR2
ADDER	MAIL	KAPO	JODSAAS	ENRT TO CDR2
UMQR	MAIL	K APO	THOMAS	MISSION COMPLETE
AFJN	FLTBD	ANAC	PIPER	RON AT ANAC
AFJN	FLTBD	MEK	DUPLISSEY	RON AT CDR2
TDC	FLTBD	ANAC	MCDANIEL	RON AT CDR2
TDC	FLTBD	ANAC	KAEMMERLING	RON AT SCANIA
TDC	FLTBD	ANAC	MAY	RON AT CDR2
TDC	FLTBD	BLD	LARVENZ	RON AT SCANIA
TDC	FLTBD	ANAC	WILLIS	RON AT CDR2
ANAC	FLTBD	AFJN	ROSE	AT NAVISTAR
TDC	FLTBD	ANAC	MODGLIN	RON AT ANAC
CDR2	FLTBD	ANAC	MORELAND	AT SCANI
ANAC	FLTBD	RDGWY	RILEY	RETURNED TO ANAC
ANAC	FLTBD	RIDGWY	MOLINA	CONVOY DID NOT ROLL
ANAC	FLTBD	RIDGWY	MONTEZ	RON AT BIAP
ANAC	FLTBD	RIDGWY	HACKLEN	RON AT TAJI
ANAC	FLTBD	RIDGWY	MORENO	AT ANAC
ANAC	FLTBD	RIDGWY	HADLEY	AT ANAC
ANAC	FLTBD	RIDGWY	GILMER	AT ANAC
ANAC	REEFER	TIKRIT	CRAIGMYLE	RON AT TKRT 4/2
ANAC	REEFER	TIKRIT	BEIER	AT TKRT
ANAC	REEFER	AFJN	SIMPSON	RON AT BIAP
FLCN	REEFER	BIAP	KROLCZYK	CMP FALCON TO BIAP
AFJN	REEFER	ANAC	LOPER	AT CDR2
******	TAJI	AIRBASE	IS CLOSED	******

KBR | KELLOGG BROWN & ROOT SERVICES INC. • LOGCAP III
CAMP ARIFJAN • KUWAIT • APO AE 09366
PHONE +965.906.1197 • DSN 825.1111

INCIDENT REPORT

Incident Report Number: 590410002.0

Date of Incident:
9 April 2004

Supervisor: Joe Jacobson

Investigation Conducted By:
KBR Safety Department, TTM
Camp Anaconda Iraq
Investigation by: Luke Singletary

Operator's Name	Licensed/Certified Trained Vehicle Operator	Assigned to	Base	Injury
Steven Fisher #298229	Yes	Tanker	Anac	Fatality
Nelson Howell #300037	Yes	Tanker	Anac	Post Traumatic Stress
James Blackwood #301384	Yes	Tanker	Anac	GSW to Rt. Foreman
Edward Sanchez #300032	Yes	Tanker	Anac	GSW to Buttocks
Danny Wood #304184	Yes	Tanker	Anac	Shrapnel wounds to left Shoulder and neck
Tommy Zimmerman #302521	Yes	Tanker	Anac	GSW to Left Lower leg
Jackie Lester #288066	Yes	Tanker	Anac	Post Traumatic Stress Large Bruise L Leg
Raymond Stennard II #304830	Yes	Tanker	Anac	Fracture to left wrist
Michael Brezovay #299901	Yes	Tanker	Anac	Post Traumatic Stress
William Peterson #300685	Yes	Tanker	Anac	Post Traumatic Stress
Randy Ross #305612	Yes	Tanker	Anac	Glass to Face (Minor)
Calvin Stanley #298297	Yes	Tanker	Anac	Shrapnel wound L. arm
Timothy Bell #282415	Yes	Tanker	Anac	Unknown/Missing
William Bradley #304683	Yes	Tanker	Anac	Unknown/Missing
Steven Hulett #300069	Yes	Tanker	Anac	Unknown/Missing
Tony Johnson #300043	Yes	Tanker	Anac	Unknown/Missing
Jeffery Parker #300012	Yes	Tanker	Anac	Unknown/Missing
Jack Montague #300645	Yes	Tanker	Anac	Unknown/Missing
Hamill Thomas #290557	Yes	Tanker	Anac	Unknown/Hostage
Ricky Tollison #303979	Yes	Tanker	Anac	No Injuries Reported

General Data Vehicle

Type Vehicle	GP Number	Property's SN Number	TTM'S Summary log	Property Damage
Freightliner	L271001	1FUYMZYB9NEP357346	1FUYMZYB9NEP357346	LDD
Freightliner	L271003	1FUYMZYB1NP357339	1FUYMZYB1NP357339	LDD
Freightliner	L271007	1FUYMZYB4NP357335	1FUYMZB4NP357335	LDD
Freightliner	L271015	1FUYMZYB3NP357357	1FUYMZYB3NP357357	LDD
Freightliner	L271021	1FUYMZYB0NP520918	1FUYMZYB0NP520918	LDD
Freightliner	L271025	1FUYMZYB0NP357350	1FUYMZYB0NP357350	LDD
Freightliner	L271028	1FUYMZYBXP357341	1FUYMZYBXNP357341	LDD
Freightliner	L271053	1FUYMZYB4NP357349	1FUYMZYB4NP357349	LDD
Freightliner	L271061	1FUYMZYB8NP357340	1FUYMZYB8NP357340	LDD
Freightliner	L271067	1FUYMZYB0NP357347	1FUYMZYB0NP357347	LDD
Freightliner	L271069	1FUYMZYB1NP357342	1FUYMZYB1N357342	LDD
Freightliner	L271071	1FUYMZYB2NP357351	1FUYMZYB2NP357351	LDD
Freightliner	L271077	1FUYMZYBXNP357369	1FUYMZYBXNP35T369	LDD

Kellogg Brown & Root Confidential Data – The information contained in this Incident Report (AIR) document may be released to the U.S. Government solely for the purpose of Contract administration and under no circumstances may this AIR or any information contained herein be released to private or third parties.

When 13th COSCOM in Anaconda suddenly announced that the roads had reopened, Stephen Pulley was skeptical. "Something smells," he wrote. I agreed and pursued further clarification with senior military command and Craig. Despite our concerns, the Hamill convoy was ultimately pushed out from Anaconda by the military. To this day, I still debate and struggle to remember whether I knew the convoy was pushed. That day was a blur—and some parts remain uncertain.

Chapter 9 All Hell Breaks Loose

A few minutes after 10 a.m., the 26-vehicle Hamill convoy rolled out—19 KBR trucks pulling camouflaged military trailers, accompanied by seven armed Humvees from the 724th Army Reserve Transportation Company. The military believed the camouflage would provide safety or act as a diversion. TTM drivers were escorted by armed soldiers. The convoy stretched nearly a mile and a half. While 25-vehicle convoys were the norm in Iraq, that length was far from ideal for force protection.

Hamill, a Mississippi dairy farmer, had assembled the vehicles at Camp Anaconda that Friday morning, unaware of the internal debates. He wasn't the kind of man to second-guess orders. "If the military pushes, we push," was the mindset. "When I went over there, I said: 'I won't refuse to go out on a mission as long as the U.S. Army is willing to escort me out,'" Hamill later said. "If they didn't want to go out, then I wouldn't go out."

Around 9:54 a.m., Lt. Col. James Carroll confirmed and approved the order sending Hamill's convoy toward Baghdad airport—right into an area where the Iraqi Mahdi Army was clashing with the Army's 1st Cavalry Division.

Three minutes later, Carroll reversed his decision and issued another email: "Sorry. It looks like [the route] is closed until further notice." However, he mistakenly sent that email only to himself. No one else received it, according to an Army report. In an interview, Carroll disputed the claim, saying he had called the military escorts to warn them not to proceed.

"When I saw I had sent the email to myself, I did everything I could to reach them," Carroll said. "It was the worst day of my life. You can't believe how much I second-guessed myself... [but] I firmly believe that I did everything I could."

Another convoy had been pushed from Anaconda before Hamill's and was attacked shortly after departure. The convoy commander made the call to turn the entire convoy around and return to Anaconda. He came to my office prior to the Hamill incident and apologized for not completing the mission. I told him he had made the right decision—and that he should be proud.

Hamill's convoy reached the junction of BIAP and Abu Ghraib prison on MSR Sword around noon on April 9. The road was already littered with burning trucks. A roadside bomb disabled Hamill's truck, forcing him to scramble for cover. He was later captured by a group of gunmen.

Other drivers pushed forward through the chaos. As bullets ripped through their cargo tanks, fuel spilled onto the, making it slick. Brakes failed. Trucks jackknifed and flipped. More IEDs detonated.

The sounds of battle crackled across the drivers' handheld radios. "I'm burning!" one driver screamed. "I'm hit, I'm hit," another called out. Telematics messages flowed from Hamill as he tried to report the situation. One of the telematics reports from Hamill is captured below.

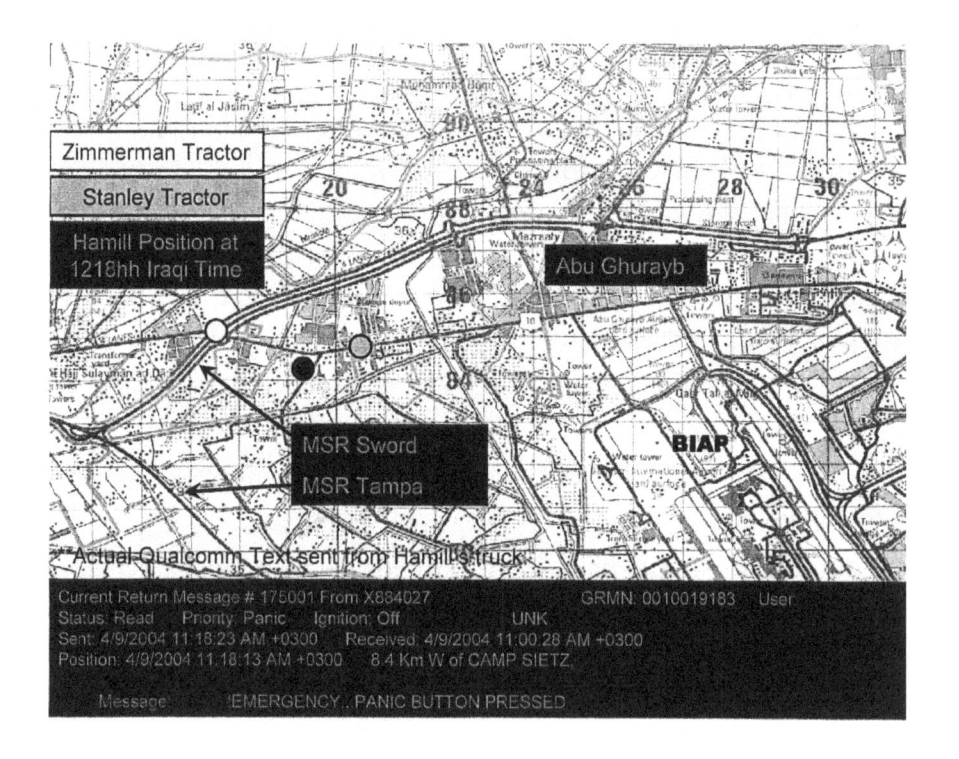

Chapter 9 All Hell Breaks Loose

In an incident report, one escort soldier wrote: "I started hearing bullets hit all over our trucks, around my head and door. They were zipping by. We pushed through the flames and kept rolling. It was just hell."

Eddie Sanchez, a driver from New Mexico, was rescued by U.S. soldiers. He recalled one soldier, visibly angry, asking, "Who are you guys? What are you doing out there? We've been fighting those guys for over 48 hours."

Randy Ross, another driver, limped into the airport with his truck riding on steel rims, his tanker and tires riddled with holes. "It was a bad day," said Ross. "A very bad day." He blamed neither KBR nor the military—he blamed Iraq.

The final toll was devastating. Six KBR drivers were killed. Most others were wounded. In addition to Hamill, who was taken hostage, another driver, Tim Bell, went missing and was presumed dead. Two soldiers were also killed. A third, Matt Maupin, was captured by insurgents and listed as missing.

Amazingly, Hamill escaped captivity after nearly three weeks. His story would later be published in his memoir *Escape in Iraq*.

Of the 19 KBR trucks in Hamill's convoy, only six reached the BIAP airport. Across Iraq that day, all 122 TTM trucks dispatched on April 9 came under attack. The harsh reality is captured in the following incident reports. The handwriting is my fragile attempt to document real time information.

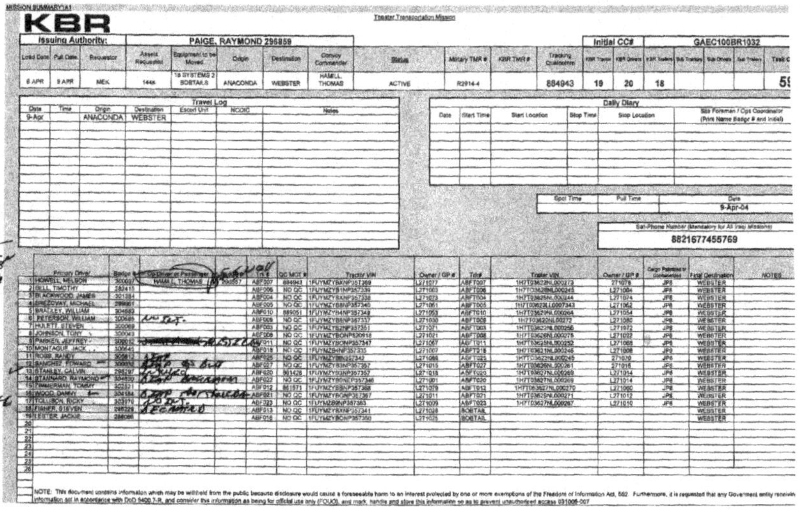

MISSION SUMMARY'A1

KBR

Theater Transportation Mission

Issuing Authority:	PAIGE, RAYMOND 296859										Initial CC#	GAEC100BR1032					
Load Date	Pull Date	Requestor	Assets Requested	Equipment to be Moved	Origin	Destination	Convoy Commander	Status	Military TMR #	KBR TMR #	Tracking Qualcomm	KBR Tractors	KBR Drivers	KBR Trailers	Sub Tractors	Sub Drivers	Sub Trailers
8 APR	9 APR	MEK	1446	18 SYSTEMS 2 BOBTAILS	ANACONDA	WEBSTER	HAMILL, THOMAS	ACTIVE	R2914-4		884943	19	20	18			

Travel Log

Date	Time	Origin	Destination	Escort Unit	NCOIC	Notes
9-Apr		ANACONDA	WEBSTER			

Daily Diary

Date	Start Time	Start Location	Stop Time	Stop Location	Site Foreman / Ops Coordinator (Print Name Badge # and Initial)

Spot Time	Pull Time	Date
		9-Apr-04

Sat-Phone Number (Mandatory for All Iraqi Missions)

8821677455769

	Primary Driver	Badge #	Co-Driver or Passenger	Badge #	Trk #	QC MOT #	Tractor VIN	Owner / GP #	Trlr#	Trailer VIN	Owner / GP #	Cargo	Final Destination	NOTES
1	HOWELL, NELSON	300037	HAMILL, THOMAS	290557	ABF007	884943	1FUYMZYBXNP357369	L271077	ABFT007	1H7T03622NL000273	271078	JP8	WEBSTER	
2	BELL, TIMOTHY	282415			ABF006	NO QC	1FUYMZYB1NP357339	L271003	ABFT006	1H7T03628NL000245	L271004	JP8	WEBSTER	
3	BLACKWOOD, JAMES	301384			ABF004	NO QC	1FUYMZYBXNP357338	L271073	ABFT004	1H7T03625NL000244	L271074	JP8	WEBSTER	
4	BREZOVAY, MICHAEL	299901			ABF005	NO QC	1FUYMZYB8NP357340	L271061	ABFT005	1H7T03623LL0007343	L271062	JP8	WEBSTER	
5	BRADLEY, WILLIAM	304683			ABF010	889051	1FUYMZYB4NP357349	L271053	ABFT010	1H7T03629NL000264	L271054	JP8	WEBSTER	
6	PETERSON, WILLIAM	300685			ABF009	NO QC	1FUYMZYB8NP357337	L271030	ABFT009	1H7T03620NL00272	L271080	JP8	WEBSTER	
7	HULETT, STEVEN	300069			ABF003	NO QC	1FUYMZYB2NP357351	L271071	ABFT003	1H7T03622NL000256	L271072	JP8	WEBSTER	
8	JOHNSON, TONY	300043			ABF008	NO QC	1FUYMZYB0NP520918	L271021	ABFT008	1H7T03626NL000275	L271022	JP8	WEBSTER	
9	PARKER, JEFFREY	300012			ABF011	NO QC	1FUYMZYB0NP357347	L271067	ABFT011	1H7T03625NL000252	L271068	JP8	WEBSTER	
10	MONTAGUE, JACK	300645			ABF018	NO QC	1FUYMZB4NP357335	L271007	ABFT018	1H7T03621NL000246	L271008	JP8	WEBSTER	
11	ROSS, RANDY	305612			ABF025	NO QC	1FUYMZYB8N357342	L271069	ABFT025	1H7T03622NL000245	271070	JP8	WEBSTER	
12	SANCHEZ, EDWARD	300032			ABF027	NO QC	1FUYMZYB3NP357357	L271015	ABFT027	1H7T03626NL000261	271016	JP8	WEBSTER	
13	STANLEY, CALVIN	298297			ABF020	861428	1FUYMZYB3NP357357	L271018	ABFT020	1H7T03627NL000269	L271014	JP8	WEBSTER	
14	STANNARD, RAYMOND	304830			ABF022	NO QC	1FUYMZYB0NEP357346	L271001	ABFT020	1H7T03627NL000269	L271014	JP8	WEBSTER	
15	ZIMMERMAN, TOMMY	302521			ABF012	861571	1FUYMZYB8NP357368	L271079	ABFT012	1H7T063627NL000270	L271060	JP8	WEBSTER	
16	WOOD, DANNY	304184			ABF021	NO QC	1FUYMZYB0NP357367	L271011	ABFT021	1H7T03625NL000271	L271012	JP8	WEBSTER	
17	TOLLISON, RICKY	303979			ABF023	NO QC	1FUYMZB9NP357363	L271009	ABFT023	1H7T03627NL000267	L271010	JP8	WEBSTER	
18	FISHER, STEVEN	298229			ABF013	NO QC	1FUYMZYBXNP357341	L271028	BOBTAIL				WEBSTER	
19	LESTER, JACKIE	288086			ABF016	NO QC	1FUYMZYB0NP357350	L271025	BOBTAIL				WEBSTER	
20														
21														
22														
23														
24														
25														
26														

NOTE: This document contains information which may be withheld from the public because disclosure would cause a foreseeable harm to an interest protected by one or more exemptions of the Freedom of Information Act, 552. Furthermore, it is requested that any Government entity receivin[g] information act in accordance with DoD 5400.7-R, and consider this information as being for official use only (FOUO), and mark, handle and store this information so as to prevent unauthorized access 031006-007

Hamill Tanker Convoy
Current Crew Status as of 29 Apr 09
Task Order 59 Anaconda to Webster

(CC) HAMILL, THOMAS	**290557**	**Captured by insurgents**
HOWELL, NELSON	300037	Uninjured, Post Traum Stress
BELL, TIMOTHY	**282415**	**Missing**
BLACKWOOD, JAMES	301384	Multiple Gunshot Wounds
BREZOVAY, MICHAEL	299901	Uninjured, Post Traum Stress
BRADLEY, WILLIAM	**304683**	**Missing**
PETERSON, WILLIAM	300685	Uninjured
HULETT, STEVEN	**300069**	**Killed in the Line of Duty**
JOHNSON, TONY	**300043**	**Killed in the Line of Duty**
PARKER, JEFFREY	**300012**	**Killed in the Line of Duty**
MONTAGUE, JACK	**300645**	**Killed in the Line of Duty**
ROSS, RANDY	305612	Uninjured
★ SANCHEZ, EDWARD	00032	Gunshot Wound
STANLEY, CALVIN	298297	Shrapnel Wounds
STENNARD, RAYMOND	304830	Broken Wrist
ZIMMERMAN, TOMMY	302521	Gunshot Wound
WOOD, DANNY	304184	Gunshot Wound
TOLLISON, RICKY	303979	Uninjured
FISHER, STEVEN	**298229**	**Killed in the Line of Duty**
LESTER, JACKIE	288086	Uninjured, Post Traum Stress

While the day remains somewhat of a blur, its memory will stay with me forever. What could we have done differently? Why were we put in that situation? My emotions, anger, and frustration were uncontrollable. At that point, my mind and body were somewhere else—beyond anything I had ever felt or experienced.

CHAPTER 10

AFTERMATH

Richard was devastated by the loss of his drivers, according to Stephen Pulley. "I thought the man was going to break down and cry after he found out he sent all those people out there," he said in a deposition. "He was very upset with himself."

Well, Pulley was right about my emotional state. But his statement that "he sent all those people out there" was grossly inaccurate. As I've said before, security had its own opinions.

That afternoon, I tried to hold our normal staff meeting with the intent of providing an update on what had happened—and maybe to consider what might come next.

It lasted only about three minutes before I broke down and abruptly left the room. Frustration, anger, and raw emotion overwhelmed me. I went to my office and cried for about 15 minutes. Italo came by and asked if he could help or if I needed anything.

"I just need time to gather myself and put everything into perspective," I told him—though I'm not sure I really understood what that meant. *What* was the perspective? I couldn't change the past. Now the past *was* my future, and it would shape the rest of my life. And what about the future for those drivers—dead, missing, or severely wounded?

Suddenly, the grim biblical story of the Slaughter of the Innocents from the Gospel of Matthew (2:16–18) came to mind. In it, Herod the Great orders the execution of all male children under two. My team—these grown men of TTM—were innocents too. The system had failed them, and it had failed me. But somehow, we all needed to find a way forward.

Right after the convoy attack, Lana and I had another emotional conversation. This time, I didn't argue. I agreed—it was time to come home. I knew then that the events of the past three days would stay with me and my family forever. I no longer had the emotional capacity to lead a large, complex organization in Iraq. And Lana was nearing a breakdown of her own. Even our two sons, who were old enough to grasp the seriousness of the situation, were shaken and worried.

Roughly an hour after that aborted staff meeting, and after reflecting on my conversation with Lana and the Bible passage, I managed to gather my thoughts and regain some composure. That marked the beginning of a new phase: managing and leading in the aftermath, for however long I remained in Iraq. I had made up my mind: *This is it. I can't do this anymore.*

Of course, it wasn't just me. The impact of April 9 reverberated across KBR, throughout the military, and ultimately across the country. The shock felt by families and communities, and the widespread *"How could this have happened?"* reaction, quickly drew attention from leadership in D.C. and Congress.

In terms of immediate action, Craig Peterson halted the TTM convoys. "No KBR convoys will move tomorrow, 10th April 04. I will inform the military chain of command," he wrote in an email. Finally, we were aligned. That gave us at least one day to assess the disaster and consider our next steps.

Chapter 10 Aftermath

Throughout the day, call after call came in—full of questions, second-guessing, and finger-pointing. I knew better than to over-communicate in writing. Given the sensitivity of the situation, limiting email correspondence helped reduce rumors and misinformation. As a senior leader within KBR, it was critical that I let corporate handle most outward communication. I instructed everyone in TTM to follow that policy. But it wasn't easy. Herding cats would've been simpler.

KBR senior leadership held daily conference calls to share status updates. Normally, these calls followed standard protocol with SITREPs covering activities and incidents. But the April 9 call was anything but standard. Everyone knew what had happened. Everyone was tense. Everyone waited for my update.

I provided a basic overview of the mission, then reported: "Three drivers were confirmed KIA and three were presumed missing. Most other drivers were wounded. Two soldiers were also KIA, and a third—Matt Maupin—is listed as missing." I heard gasps on the line. Someone muttered an angry "shit." I'm not sure who said it, but it captured the mood. "Shit" was exactly what it was.

The call was led by a Senior KBR official in Houston—the head of the Government Contracting Division, a retired Admiral if I recall correctly. After my update, he asked several questions and made one particular comment: "We need to refrain from using the term KIA. That's a military reference and implies civilians were in combat."

My first thought? *Really? Want me to call them roadkill instead?* I was in a "don't give a damn" mindset. It felt like some of KBR's leadership had no concept of the reality we were dealing with. But I stayed composed and continued the call.

In the end, seven drivers were killed: William Bradley, Timothy Bell, Stephen Hulett, Steven Scott Fisher, Tony Duane Johnson,

Jack Montague, and Jeffrey Parker. Bradley and Bell were initially classified as missing. Bradley's remains were recovered in 2005. Bell's remains were never found.

Of course, KBR did everything it could to provide information to the families of the Hamill convoy drivers. It was an extremely sensitive situation, requiring careful coordination with both military leadership and our communications staff. We knew the facts, but not all of them could or should be shared right away. Some were best handled by corporate and our military customers as they investigated what went wrong.

Leaking any information, true or not, could fuel the media frenzy and hurt the very people we were trying to support—the survivors and the families of those injured, missing, or killed. If left unchecked, that information could spiral out of control and lose all context.

The KBR legal team got involved almost immediately. That's when I first met Sharron Stagg, Assistant General Counsel. She's now retired, but she was widely respected across KBR and the industry. Sharron and I would become close confidants—and we're still in touch to this day. Her guidance was invaluable. She brought not only legal expertise but also a much-needed human touch to the chaos we were facing.

After that day that would live in infamy, I sat alone in my office and living quarters on the evening of April 9th, thinking, *"I will be living with this for a very long time."* Just outside my walls, the Iraqi insurgency raged on. U.S. troops were dangerously low on everything they needed. And *my* drivers—some literally licking their wounds, others no doubt still in shock—needed support. They needed me to translate what I was seeing and hearing, to help them understand what we had signed on to do together, and to offer my read on the situation so they could make their own decisions.

Chapter 10 Aftermath

The most important part of my responsibility now was meeting with them—speaking with them face to face. As exhausted as I was, sleep didn't come easily. But eventually, it did. We had April 10th to regroup and try to continue supporting the troops. Welcome to another day in Iraq.

April 9 was now behind us, but I wasn't sure I could pull myself together enough to stand in front of 100+ people and say anything coherent. After some time, I did what any leader must do: I strapped on my boots and got it together—partly on autopilot, and partly with the love of my family carrying me through the day.

As I stood in front of the drivers, it was a surreal moment. Many of them were angry and uncertain and had every right to be. I needed to deliver a message rooted in truth, compassion, and reality. This was no time for platitudes or corporate speak. The drivers listened, and most understood. They knew Iraq was dangerous. They knew things weren't going according to plan. There were many questions—it felt almost like a therapy session. Real people talking about real things. A welcome shift from some of the bureaucratic nonsense I'd been dealing with.

Of course, I didn't have all the answers. But I did my best to convey confidence and reality. I assured them we were working with the military, conducting after-action assessments, and doing everything we could to get the support needed to continue our missions. It was good for them, and probably for me, to have these issues aired and to know someone was listening.

Surprisingly, a small percentage of drivers resigned. Many were ready, and even eager, to get back out there. They had come to see their work as something more than just a paycheck. These were true heroes and patriots. Their commitment stirred my deepest emotions. What had happened was painful and unimaginable, but here they were saying, *We can do this. We're still in.* Their passion and courage were extraordinary.

The following is a handwritten account of the driver attrition from April 9 through the end of April 2004.

```
TTM Attrition since 4/9

              ANAC    CEDAR    Kuwait
DRIVER         43        7        16      66

OTHERS         12        0         0      12
              ___      ___      ___
               55        7        16
```

At that moment, I was deeply proud to be part of a team that believed in our country and was completely committed to supporting the troops. But for better or worse, their courage and resolve would soon be tested again.

After several meetings and conference calls, the military and KBR leadership reached an agreement to resume operations. The convoy attack had affected not just fuel transport by KBR, but also the delivery of ammunition, food for the DFACs, and other essential supplies. The DFACs were running low. For several days, the menu consisted of basics: meat, eggs, bread, chicken, mashed potatoes... and of course, MREs. That's when I became familiar with MRE desserts.

The situation had dramatically shifted from the minimal escort that had accompanied the Hamill convoy. Now, it was full-scale force protection for our civilians. Anything less was off the table. Our convoys were essential to continuing the fight against the insurgents and to keeping the troops supplied. The insurgents knew this—cutting off our supply lines was a clear tactic. For the military, it was win or lose.

Chapter 10 Aftermath

The Army decided maximum protection was needed for convoys north of Baghdad and in and out of Anaconda. That's when I was introduced to the "Strykers." These eight-wheeled, all-wheel drive armored vehicles were designed to support infantry, bring firepower to combat, and "take the fight to the enemy." Fast, versatile, and heavily armed, they could carry up to nine soldiers ready for battle. The military told me, *these will protect your convoys*.

Here we go again. "Take the fight to the enemy"? That sounded dangerously familiar—like a repeat of what happened on April 9, only with heavier firepower. I understood the need for increased protection, but this felt like we were once again being dragged onto a battlefield.

After many discussions with military and KBR leadership, it was decided that convoys would resume movement on April 11. This time, the military would be smarter about routes and timing. They desperately needed JP8 to fuel Humvees, tanks, trucks—everything. We met with the drivers and asked for volunteers.

As before, bravery and patriotism showed up. Many raised their hands, ready to continue. On the morning of April 11, I walked around the convoy staging area and thanked them personally for their commitment. Many said, *"F" those bastards. We're not going to let them win."*

I also walked among the Strykers—urban war machines. The soldiers were more than ready to fight. I reminded military leadership again: this wasn't about taking civilians into battle. It was about using a show of force to prevent another fight from breaking out.

That day, convoys moved out of Anaconda under Stryker protection and delivered desperately needed fuel to Baghdad and other locations. The military wisely kept us off the MSRs, opting for alternate routes. One small convoy out of Camp Cedar, escorted by Humvees, delivered JP8 to a forward operating base in southeast Iraq. As soon as the trucks arrived, troops began fueling up directly from the tankers.

In civilian supply chain terms, it was "just-in-time" (JIT) delivery. But a Hollywood screenwriter would've called it what it was: *just in the nick of time.*

As the days passed—though "normal" was a stretch—KBR convoys resumed a routine of daily missions. The Strykers were soon pulled from our protection detail. The optics weren't good: civilians escorted by front-line war machines made us look like we were embedded in a combat unit. And whether or not they were beside us, we were still on a battlefield. But there was no question the military was doing its best to prioritize our safety.

The events of April 9 lingered. In an email to an Army general after the attack, Craig Peterson asked: *"Do you think there was any way we could have predicted the events of 8/9 April—the convoy hits? Do you think we had any real predictive intel or warnings that would have led us to halt movement?"*

It was Monday morning quarterbacking, yes, but the deeper question was clear: *Why were civilians on a battlefield in the first place?* Craig ultimately resigned from his role not long after.

TTM Security Manager Stephen Pulley was unequivocal: *"KBR security did their job."* And: *"KBR security was overruled."* We were all angry, emotional, and frustrated. The bottom line was this: civilians were operating on a military battlefield, under military direction, and lives were lost.

The military conducted its own investigation into the April 9 attack. The resulting 280-page report concluded that miscommunications about road danger contributed to the casualties. No kidding. I could've summarized that in one page.

The investigating officer noted he wasn't allowed to examine the actions of military officials in the 13th COSCOM because they were outside his chain of command. A thoroughly unsatisfying conclusion, to say the least.

Chapter 10 Aftermath

In a later court ruling, District Judge Gray Miller—who was involved in litigation related to the April 9 incident—wrote: *"Is it wise to use civilian contractors in a war zone? Was it wise to send the convoy along the route [to Baghdad airport] on April 9, 2004?"* His conclusion: *"Answering either question, or the many in between, would require the court to examine wartime policies of the executive branch—a step the court declines to take."*

No one was denying that civilians were in the line of fire. But the Department of Defense, relying on long-standing SOPs built around traditional wars, had deemed this a "peacetime rebuilding effort."

But there *was* no peace in the Middle East—certainly not then, and not now. And as I expected, I remained at the center of it all.

CHAPTER 11

HOME ON THE SHOOTING RANGE

Lana and I had made a concrete decision: I was coming home to Texas as soon as possible. I communicated this to Houston Ray and Craig. Ray understood, but he asked if I'd take a few days to think it over. Was there really anything to think about? Everything in my civilian supply chain world had gone wrong. Brave drivers had been sent into harm's way. Some killed, many wounded. And all of us were hurting in one way or another. I was no longer in the right mindset to continue the fiction of a "peacetime operation" in the middle of a war zone. Uncle Sam still had unfinished business, but as far as I was concerned, I was done.

I knew I had valuable experience leading large and complex supply chain operations—experience that was needed in the Middle East. But at this stage, the most critical leadership trait seemed to be the ability to navigate military bureaucracy. And I was over it. Houston Ray and I spoke again a day or two later, and after additional conversations with Craig and other members of KBR leadership, they made me an unexpected offer: remain in my leadership role but relocate permanently to Kuwait.

Lana and I had both made up our minds, and changing course would be difficult—especially convincing her. We spoke later that day about the offer. We weighed various options, including the possibility of her visiting Kuwait in May to ease her concerns. After a long conversation, we decided to sleep on it and revisit the discussion in the morning.

Lana was frustrated and eventually landed in an "it's your decision" mindset—but only if I stayed in Kuwait. She tried to convince herself that this was a workable compromise. She cited examples—like getting hit by a bus in the U.S. or something tragic happening to me in Iraq or Kuwait—as a reminder that none of us can predict the future. Danger existed everywhere.

With that partial blessing, and my own sense of unfinished business—leaving TTM completely high and dry felt unprofessional, maybe even un-American. I told Ray I would stay under two conditions. First, I wanted to remain in Kuwait, which, frankly, was what I thought I had signed up for in the first place. Second, I wanted permission for Lana to visit Kuwait in May. Because LOGCAP was a DoD operation, there was initial hesitation about family members in theater—certainly not in Iraq—but Ray worked his magic. The KBR contract team approved Lana's visit, with the understanding we'd keep a low profile. We were bending some DoD rules, and more delicately, had to respect Kuwaiti and Muslim cultural norms.

With that agreement in place, Lana and I decided I would remain in my role with TTM through the end of my one-year contract, and then we'd reevaluate our future. Kuwait would serve as a down payment on the next phase of our lives.

I transitioned back to Kuwait in late April. But before I left Iraq, I knew we needed to fill the DPM role in Anaconda with someone strong and trustworthy. I already knew who I wanted: Art—one of the Three Amigos. Since I now had more control over personnel decisions, I was adamant. I received pushback from several senior KBR executives and even from a few military leaders

Chapter 11 Home on the Shooting Range

who knew Art. But I stood firm: Art and I were a package deal. He might not have checked every box on the official leadership checklist, but he checked the three that mattered to me: truthfulness, trustworthiness, and integrity.

Alongside James in Kuwait and British Ray on the admin side, Art would complete the triad I needed—three people I could count on to tell me the truth, not just what they thought I wanted to hear.

After a couple of days, Houston Ray and the KBR executive staff agreed to promote Art to DPM in Anaconda. I had a conversation with the current DPM, explained the transition plan, and gave him the option to resign and stay through May to ensure a smooth handoff.

With Art and Italo in place, I felt comfortable with the situation in Iraq. They'd be my eyes and ears. From Kuwait, I could now focus on the big picture—our supply chain foundation and strategic leadership.

My final two weeks at Anaconda were all about redefining "normal" for me and for the team. April 9 had changed everything, and we weren't the same. But I knew it was my job to help others interpret what came next. I was low on enthusiasm, but I still wanted to stabilize our relationship with military leadership and reassure our drivers and support staff that they were seen, valued, and backed by management.

I continued regular meetings with the operations team, drivers, and military officers. Chris Andrews and I kept up our breakfast meetings. He was a friend and someone I could speak with honestly about what April 9 had done to me and to the team. His perspective was always valuable. I also spoke with Lt. Col. Davidson. She was empathetic and expressed her commitment to helping TTM push forward and support both the mission and the people.

As I boarded the C-130 at Anaconda and strapped in—flights out were as chaotic as flights in—I felt emotionally drained, running on empty. How would I lead TTM from Kuwait? What would the military think of my departure? I was anxious and frustrated, second-guessing myself, and silently berating the choices that had led to this no-win scenario.

There was a sense of relief as we lifted off. But when the C-130 touched down at Camp Arifjan in Kuwait, all the anxiety I had tried to suppress came rushing back. It was like nothing I had experienced before—or since. Though I could see the tarmac and knew we were back on the ground, it felt like an out-of-body experience. The tension, worry, internal conflict—it all swirled inside me. My head was spinning. My body felt weak. My mind was somewhere else.

British Ray and James were there to greet me. They probably noticed I was spaced out. James, with all his military experience, had likely seen that look before. But they were my team, and they wanted to help. I asked them to take me straight to my living quarters so I could collect myself.

Since I had "permanently" relocated to Anaconda, James had moved into my private quarters. Ever the soldier, he was ready to give it back to me. I declined. Being in a multi-room condo with other staff would be better. I needed some small talk and routine—something that didn't involve immediate decisions about MSRs or chain-of-command issues. We returned to the same resort area as before. James, Ray and I unloaded my things, and Art joined us later in the afternoon. We talked for hours—mostly about April 8th and 9th.

Art and I also spent time discussing his upcoming transition. I reassured him that he had my full support. He might not have checked every box KBR leadership was looking for, but I knew he was more than capable of leading the team.

The next morning arrived quickly. I gathered my gear and rode to Arifjan with James and Ray. And there—another surprise. A pleasant one. The TTM operation had grown into a full office complex made up of several 20'x10' trailers. I looked at them and said, "What the F?" They both grinned. "We made some changes, boss man."

"Boss man" had become a nickname. James started it, and it caught on.

As we pulled into the complex and walked toward my new office, I could tell the staff didn't quite know how to act. Everyone was on edge, unsure of what to say. What do you say to someone who's lost multiple people under their command? Just like in Houston during orientation, I felt like a marked man—an object of quiet discussion.

I carried a lot of emotional baggage, but I had a job to do and so did they. So, I walked around and tried to greet everyone. Things weren't 100% normal, but we were still a team.

My new office was a shared space with James. It was a great setup. We could talk openly about work, and when I needed silence, he knew to give me space. Conversation came easily between us, and that helped.

And James still had his reputation. One day, a truck driver entered our office unannounced and tried to start a conversation. James snapped into action like a guided missile. "You do not enter the office of the PM without an appointment or at least knocking. Show some respect!"

The driver froze, then slunk away. I sheepishly told James it was okay. "No, boss man," he said. "They need to respect your position."

He was right, but I wasn't feeling it. I felt distant from others. Vaguely confused. Angry, though I couldn't quite pinpoint at what. I had always been tough, but now I was a different kind of hard-ass with an extremely short fuse. I had zero tolerance for incompetence. It was my way or the highway, and the staff knew it. Conversations were brief and strictly business. I wasn't in the mood for nonsense. James protected me like a bodyguard—deflecting annoyances and giving me breathing room.

For the first time in my life, I was taking things day by day. My goals were simple: eat, work, sleep, exercise, and focus on the next event—nothing more. That next event was what kept me going. During this stretch, the next really big event was Lana's visit to Kuwait. We scheduled her trip for mid-May. I couldn't quite picture it, but I was sure it would be good. She was flying into Kuwait City, and I'd arranged for a private room away from the staff. I had already prepped her on Muslim culture and customs.

When she came through security, we embraced with a very light hug. Remember—we were in Kuwait. Public displays of affection between men and women are impermissible in Muslim culture. While Islam doesn't forbid natural human interaction between the sexes, public or social physical touch is off-limits. After that moment, we were careful to respect and abide by the cultural expectations.

We drove to our room—a quaint little living space—and once we were inside, we embraced properly. Emotions took over. We cried and talked for hours. It was a relief to see her in this environment. Her presence brought me a sense of normalcy, a reminder that there was still a world beyond TTM, Kuwait, and Iraq.

We made the most of our time in Kuwait. I got her a temporary badge so she could visit Camp Arifjan. It wasn't exactly the highlight of our trip, but it gave her a "slice of life" perspective. That said, it came with its own learning curve. When we walked into the DFAC for lunch, the military guard stopped us. Lana couldn't enter because she was wearing a sleeveless shirt. It was 110 degrees, and she was dressed appropriately for the heat. I had forgotten that military protocol requires shoulders to be covered in public facilities. My mistake. We grabbed burgers from the Hardee's on base instead.

Another moment underscored just how different life was in a Muslim country. We went to a nice restaurant in Kuwait City—upscale, with a mix of local and American cuisine. When the waiter arrived, he wouldn't look at Lana or acknowledge her presence.

Chapter 11 Home on the Shooting Range

She tried to order her meal, but he wouldn't respond. I had to place her order for her. After he walked away, she said, "I would not survive in this culture and the men around me wouldn't either." I just nodded. Yep. But when in Rome—or Kuwait—we had to go with the flow.

We also traveled to Dubai. What an experience. Opulence was everywhere. We were picked up at the airport in a Mercedes, pretty standard for Dubai. We arrived at the resort, jaws practically on the floor. The amenities, the decor—it was overwhelming. We stayed at the Jumeirah Beach Hotel, which complements the famous sail-shaped Burj Al Arab across the way. This was the same property where, just a few months earlier, Tiger Woods had hit golf balls off the Burj's helipad.

When we checked in, the concierge said, "Welcome, Mr. Richard. We've been expecting you. We upgraded your room." Lana and I looked at each other, then around at the luxury surrounding us, and thought, *Upgrade?* I'd contacted a procurement director I knew from Halliburton's Dubai team to help with our booking. Clearly, he had connections.

Outside the hotel, we were guided to what I can only describe as an upscale canoe—a narrow, human-powered boat maybe twelve to fourteen feet long. The escort greeted us: "Welcome, Mr. and Mrs. Richard. Please take a seat. I'll take you to your room." We nearly burst out laughing but went with it. He paddled us to a beachside cabana that turned out to be the most over-the-top room either of us had ever seen—marble tub and sink, intricate flooring, fresh flowers, and every amenity imaginable. We were right on the beach. Anything we needed was just a phone call away. I hadn't realized we'd be right on the water, so I had to buy swim trunks and flip-flops from the hotel. Lana, of course, came prepared.

July 7, 2004, marked our 20-year anniversary, so I decided to buy her a diamond ring while in Dubai. The city is known for its high-quality jewelry at prices well below U.S. norms. Better yet, you can negotiate. I visited a shop recommended by my Halliburton contact. Lana had no idea. When we arrived, she found a ring she loved. After nearly an hour of bargaining, we got it for half the original asking price. Later, back in the States, the ring appraised for double what we paid. She still wears it.

Dubai was a dream and a real escape from TTM. For the first time in a long while, I felt almost normal. One of the highlights was visiting the Burj Al Arab itself. We had drinks at the bar on the top floor nearly 700 feet above the Persian Gulf. The views were breathtaking. The entire trip felt surreal. Anything and everything we could possibly want was available within the resort. The only time we left was to buy the ring. But, like all good dreams, it had to end.

We took the same flight back. I disembarked in Kuwait, ready to face more chaos. Lana continued ahead to the U.S. Our goodbye was a little easier this time, as we already anticipated our next visit.

We'd decided I would return to the U.S. in June, and the thought of coming home kept me energized and focused. But in the time between Dubai and my planned departure, a few unexpected developments occurred.

As I transitioned into the leadership role in Kuwait, thoughts of April 9th came back in waves. What did it all mean? Would I ever make peace with it? I couldn't stop thinking about what we might have done differently. Hindsight is 20/20, but even now, with all the analysis, I never had an "aha" moment—no clear decision point where a different choice would've changed the outcome. Outwardly, I was short-tempered. Inwardly, I was still reeling. I shared some of my feelings with family and friends, through emails and conversations, but looking back, I think it was more than they knew how to handle.

Routine helped: work, food, sleep. Those rhythms made the days bearable. But even as I talked with family as much as ever, I was beginning to drift emotionally—becoming more distant, even

Chapter 11 Home on the Shooting Range

from Lana. I started identifying more with the TTM organization. They were there with me. They understood. They were becoming my family. And like any family forged under pressure, we clung to small comforts and quick escapes—ways to fill the void left by all we had lost.

I wasn't quite one of the "good ol' boys," but I was definitely starting to think like a career contractor. We were strangers in a strange land, united by our losses, our frustrations, and a shared determination to survive. But not everyone played by the rules.

One morning, British Ray and I were driving to the KBR admin offices when I noticed about 100 flatbed trailers parked in the TTM equipment staging area.

"What the F is that?" I shouted.

Ray responded, "What, boss man?"

"The flatbeds. I didn't approve any flatbed leases."

Ray's reply: "Okay, okay—I'll run it down."

A few hours later, Ray returned with a copy of a Request for Purchase (RFP)—with my name on it. Problem was, it wasn't my signature. I'd signed a Request for Quote (RFQ), not an RFP. Even worse, the RFP was for an $11 million lease—above my $10 million signature authority.

Turns out, the RFP had been executed by the same acquaintance of the terminated transportation manager who now worked for the flatbed leasing company that reported to British Ray. We knew karma was going to happen. Someone had forged my name. We immediately notified KBR Security. After a short investigation, the staffer was terminated. As for what happened to her and the former manager... I'll let your imagination fill in the blanks.

And then, because this whole experience needed one more absurd twist, I started receiving threatening text messages: *I'm going to kill you... You're being watched... Watch your back.*

Again, I called KBR Security. They brought in the Kuwaiti Police. Another *surprise, surprise, surprise*. The messages were coming from the phone of the terminated transportation manager. He was picked up and taken to the Kuwait City police station. Apparently, he thought *what happens in Kuwait stays in Kuwait*. Not quite.

Security and the police asked if I wanted to press charges. I didn't. I had bigger things to focus on. He was a piece of shit, and I knew the ongoing investigations would eventually catch up with him. Just another entry in the growing file of "you-can't-make-this-shit-up" moments from my one-year contract.

At the other end of the spectrum, leadership was shifting again. KBR replaced Craig with a retired three-star general—clearly a strategic move. The idea was that someone with high rank would be able to navigate the DoD bureaucracy and command attention from military leaders in theater. A Three Star would be hard to ignore.

In my mind, these rent-a-generals were still civilians. The Three Star was no exception. I respected his service and would offer my full professional support, but I wasn't going to let military rank translate to undue civilian authority. I knew the supply chain inside and out, globally and on the ground, and wasn't going to be steamrolled by brass.

The bigger challenge came in the form of the next leadership hire: a retired brigadier general—One Star. I wasn't sure where he fell in the chain of command, but from day one, we clashed. It wasn't clear if I reported to him or to the Three Star, and no one seemed interested in clarifying. One Star was constantly in my business, seemingly intent on dismantling TTM. I made it clear—via email and conversation—that I wasn't going to put up with it. He didn't understand logistics, didn't understand TTM, and contributed nothing useful to our mission. He was a royal pain in my ass.

Chapter 11 Home on the Shooting Range

At one point, I learned he'd been riding in trucks with TTM postal drivers in Baghdad. I was floored. What the hell was that about? It was irresponsible, dangerous, and totally unnecessary. Our drivers already had enough to worry about without some brass hat wedging himself into the cab.

We had a "come to Jesus" meeting, and I also spoke directly with the Three Star. I made it crystal clear: no one rides in TTM trucks without my knowledge or the TOC's approval. One Star and I would continue our back-and-forth skirmishes for the rest of my tenure. To this day, I still don't know what his purpose was, or what he thought he was achieving. Just another riddle buried in the sands of the Middle East.

CHAPTER 12

THE FALLOUT AND WOUNDS YOU CAN'T SEE

Anxiety, frustration, and anger had become my new normal. And amidst all of that, one event stood out as a source of deep, lingering regret.

As the days and weeks passed, I tried to navigate through the emotional wreckage of April 9 while staying focused on leading TTM. I was anticipating a visit home to the U.S.—a much-needed break. Then I received unexpected news: a Congressional Hearing with the House Government Reform Committee was scheduled for July in Washington, D.C.

Halliburton and KBR were under constant partisan scrutiny regarding the LOGCAP III contract. Several Congressional Hearings had already been held on various topics—many of them triggered by whistleblowers eager for their moment in the spotlight. For the July hearing, Halliburton and KBR executives began selecting potential candidates to represent the operational side of running such a massive and complex organization in the Middle East. One anticipated focus was the use of civilians on a battlefield.

KBR asked if I would be interested in serving as one of those candidates. I was caught completely off guard—surprised, humbled, and a little shaken. The kid from South Mississippi hadn't expected a call like that. But I knew I had seen and learned a lot "in theater," and believed I could offer a valuable, on-the-ground perspective.

Though I wasn't certain what topics would be covered in the hearing, I was clear on one thing: I wanted a forum to share the truth about the TTM mission. And what a forum this was. I accepted the opportunity without hesitation and called Lana that afternoon to share the news. We were both pleasantly surprised and understood the magnitude of the opportunity.

The trip home, of course, wasn't without its own drama—but this time it had nothing to do with insurgents or supply chain dysfunction.

The morning I was scheduled to leave for the U.S., I got a call from Lana. She and our youngest son, Aaron, had just been in a serious car accident. Earlier that year, we had bought a travel trailer and a Chevy Suburban. Lana enjoyed "glamping"—the term for camping in an RV or trailer rather than roughing it in a tent. She wasn't, and still isn't, a "tent" person.

The trailer had been stored at a facility about 30 miles north of our home. Lana and Aaron were driving it back in preparation for our upcoming trip during my time at home. Somewhere along the route, the trailer jackknifed on a bridge, struck the embankment, and both the trailer and Suburban flipped. The Suburban detached, rolled three times, and landed upside down on the highway.

Lana called me from the ambulance. You can imagine the panic that washed over me—another gut punch added to everything I was already carrying. She had also contacted our close friends, Joanne and Kevin. After speaking with Lana, I called them to ask for updates. Joanne was already on her way to the hospital. Friends like that are a blessing.

Chapter 12 The Fallout and Wounds You Can't See

Both Lana and Aaron were examined at a local hospital and—thank God—were spared serious injury. Joanne and Kevin later told me they had some bumps and bruises but were otherwise okay. After all I'd seen happen to my TTM drivers, that news felt like a miracle. The Suburban and trailer were totaled, but I was deeply grateful they were safe.

With a quiet sigh of relief, I flew home—thankful, emotional, and still trying to process it all.

Arriving home was surreal. It felt like I'd only just left, and also like I'd been gone a hundred years. Seeing Lana and Aaron, especially knowing they were truly okay, was a joy. I visited with family and friends, and Lana hosted a welcome-home party. It was wonderful—laughter, food, and the kind of warm camaraderie I hadn't felt in months.

We only had one vehicle at the time—just what Lana had been using. After the accident, we both agreed that the Suburban's size likely played a big role in their survival, so we wanted another large vehicle. But Lana wasn't ready to drive another Suburban. We compromised and bought a Nissan Titan truck instead.

Even while I was home, KBR's request for the Congressional Hearing kept TTM at the forefront of my mind. Because I'd be in D.C. for a couple of weeks, we decided to turn it into a short family vacation. While still home, Lana and I scheduled flights for her and the boys to meet me there. It was another chance for us to reconnect and share time as a family.

The visit home flew by. Before I knew it, I was heading back to Kuwait. I wasn't looking forward to it, but at the same time, I never really felt like I'd left. My return flight routed through Amsterdam. As I sat on the plane, my thoughts drifted right back to the same place: anger, frustration, and emotional emptiness. *Here we go again. What's next?*

The next few weeks were focused on settling back into the rhythm of work in Kuwait. James let me know he was planning to take R&R after my trip to D.C.—and that he was considering resigning. It was hard to hear, but I understood. I asked him to let me know as soon as possible, and about a week later, he confirmed his decision.

I immediately began reaching out to trusted contacts in KBR for recommendations. To my surprise, Lt. Col. Sue Davidson contacted me about a retired Army Chief Warrant Officer who might be a good fit for the DPM role. Warrant Officers occupy a unique place in the chain of command. They are ranked above enlisted personnel and officer candidates, and their job is to manage, operate, and maintain complex systems and functions across all operational areas.

I had deep respect for Sue's judgment and gave the candidate a call. After a week of discussions, he agreed to take the position. He was set to start the week before my D.C. trip, which gave him time to onboard with me and overlap with James for a proper handoff.

Regret

Regret is a feeling of sadness, repentance, or disappointment over something that has happened or been done. Over the past seven months with TTM, there were plenty of opportunities where I might have felt regret over decisions I made, actions I took, or outcomes that spiraled beyond anyone's control. But truthfully, while I was deeply frustrated and often angry, I didn't carry regret for most of those choices. I stood by my decisions, even when the outcomes were tragic.

This part of the story, however, is something I debated sharing—even with myself. It goes beyond the formal narrative of TTM and the war we found ourselves unwillingly dragged into. I spoke about it with a couple of close friends, most often with my friend Bill. Bill has been a sounding board for years. He was one

Chapter 12 The Fallout and Wounds You Can't See

of those who inspired me to write this book. Throughout 2024, during the 20-year anniversary of those events, we talked regularly. He kept urging me to move forward and tell the whole story.

There was one topic, though—one very personal and painful truth—that I struggled to include. It was emotionally loaded, full of shame, and the hardest part to explain to people in my life who weren't aware. It was also one of the reasons I delayed writing this book for so long.

Through prayer, reflection, and long conversations with Lana, I came to believe that it was important to include it—not to justify, but to be honest. This story wouldn't be complete without it. It speaks to the depth of the emptiness and disconnection I felt during that time. But it also speaks to forgiveness, faith, and the resilience of commitment. It was our shared faith in the Lord—and, eventually, in each other—that carried us through.

The truth is, I was unfaithful. I had an affair.

She worked in the press department for Halliburton, helping create a story about TTM. We met during a briefing in Kuwait prior to my trip to Washington, D.C. We had dinner before the trip. The affair began after I returned to Kuwait.

By then, I had become almost completely disconnected from the normal rhythms of everyday life. As I mentioned earlier, my mindset had shifted. I had become—emotionally and mentally—a "contractor." I was living at the edges of American life, connected but disconnected. Detached. In conversations with Lana, I often referred to the TTM staff as *family*. I said things like, *"This is my family now."* At the time, I didn't realize just how much that statement revealed.

Lana, ever patient and trying her best to remain hopeful, felt the growing strain. Our relationship suffered. In hindsight, I was a lost soul—adrift, losing touch with the anchors that had always held me steady: family, friends, and faith. The chaotic, pressure-filled world of TTM had become my reality. It felt real. Everything back home, by contrast, felt distant and hard to explain.

The weeks leading up to the D.C. trip were filled with meetings, preparations, and nonstop stress about the hearing. That process demanded my full attention, and the emotional walls I had been building kept getting higher. Looking back, I understand the pain I caused, and I carry that with me.

But more than that, I carry the grace that followed. Lana and I made it through. Not without scars, but with honesty, repentance, and work. Faith saved us. Forgiveness saved us. And in the end, our commitment to each other proved stronger than even the worst version of ourselves.

Congressional Hearing

I let Lana know ahead of time that I wouldn't have much time to spend with her and the boys during the D.C. trip, but I promised to do my best. I was going to be the public face of KBR, whether for better or worse, and that responsibility left little room for distraction. I may have been wearing a suit and tie, but mentally, I was still hunkered down at Camp Anaconda, listening for the alarm to head to shelter.

Lana and the boys made the most of the trip, visiting museums and historical sights. I was able to break away briefly a couple of times for some sightseeing and dinners together. I was grateful for those moments, though I was distracted every step of the way.

The hearing preparation was long, detailed, and exhausting. KBR and Halliburton executives, legal teams, and consultants led us through day after day of briefings. It was 12-hour days of mock hearings, rehearsed questions—both friendly and adversarial—and detailed coaching. By the end of the first week, I was officially

Chapter 12 The Fallout and Wounds You Can't See

selected as one of four individuals to testify. That's when it became real.

We were briefed on everything from how to speak, what not to say, how to maintain composure, even how to dress. The dress code was specific: a dark gray or navy suit and a plain, unassuming tie.

The second week was even more intense. We went through multiple mock hearings, drilling every detail. There were two actual hearings before ours—one featuring whistleblowers and another with KBR procurement staff. The official Congressional hearing took place on July 22, 2004, before the House Government Reform Committee.

The committee was chaired by Representative Tom Davis of Virginia's 11th congressional district. On the other side of the aisle was Representative Henry Waxman, a Democrat from California's 30th district—which included areas like West Hollywood, Santa Monica, and Beverly Hills. Waxman was widely known as one of the most outspoken and influential liberal members of Congress. In 2007, following the Democrats' midterm victory, he became Chairman and added "House Oversight" to the committee's name.

We entered the hearing room and took our seats. It looked just like the scenes you see on C-SPAN with cameras rolling, journalists in the room, staffers and aides positioned in the back rows, and committee members drifting in and out. The hearing was being broadcast live on C-SPAN.

Earlier that day, a separate hearing had featured three former KBR employees from the whistleblower group—two of them former TTM truck drivers who had been terminated. They came in with an axe to grind.

Chairman Davis summed up the situation clearly:

"After a preliminary evaluation, we agreed to a hearing involving some of the whistleblowers, only to see that the whistleblower statements were on the Democrats' website, which also led to the appropriate television news interviews—all without any concern for the validity of the statements. In other words, the minority was more concerned with sensational accusations getting to the media than with the actual fact-finding this committee is equipped to conduct."

Representative Waxman followed up with the Democrats' position, highlighting alleged waste, abuse, and fraud in LOGCAP operations. To me, it all sounded like typical Washington partisan theatrics.

The two terminated truck drivers claimed that trucks had been abandoned on the MSRs without attempts to recover them, and that fleet maintenance was nonexistent. I knew I'd be addressing all of that shortly.

KBR's witness list for the day included:

Alfred Jeffgen, Chief Operating Officer, KBR Government Operations – Americas Region

William Walter, Director of Government Compliance, KBR Government Operations

Charles "Stoney" Cox, Vice President and former RIO (Restore Iraqi Oil) Project Director

And me: Keith Richard, Regional Project Manager, Theater Transportation Mission (TTM), LOGCAP III

Each of us provided opening statements before facing questions from the committee.

My Opening Statement

I am the KBR Government Operations Regional Project Manager for the Theater Transportation Mission in Iraq and Kuwait. In this role, I oversee all KBR LOGCAP transportation missions in Iraq and Kuwait.

Chapter 12 The Fallout and Wounds You Can't See

I'm pleased to address the committee on a key role KBR is playing to help support our troops in Iraq. In addition to the trucks that supplied Iraqi civilians with fuel, KBR also initiated a separate program to support the delivery of military fuel, parts, food, and mail to coalition forces. Thus far, KBR trucks have driven nearly forty million miles and completed over 128,000 deliveries.

We operate a fleet of approximately 2,000 trucks, staffed by 1,700 drivers, 300 mechanics, logistics specialists, clerks, and heavy equipment operators. In terms of miles driven and fleet size, we are the equivalent of the fourth-largest trucking company in the United States—and we stood up that capability in a matter of months.

> Let me take you through a typical trip, if typical is the right word. Our trucks typically traveled from Kuwait to the central distribution center at Camp Anaconda and back. A distance of 1,100 miles round trip in a States trip, equivalent of travel from Richmond to Boston, would take 2 days, or 9 hours up and 9 hours back. But in Iraq it is almost a 5 or even a 6-day trip, and that's if all goes well. On the run to Camp Anaconda, the driver's day begins with a pre-trip inspection of his truck and trailer in Kuwait followed by a meeting with the latest security briefing.
>
> The mood is tense, and I certainly know that in trips I have made, my adrenalin is pumping. Trucks are joined by military escorts at the Iraqi border. From there they travel to Camp Cedar, a support center, where they remain overnight. The next day a new set of escorts joins in to head on to Scania, a massive truck stop where yet other escort awaits.
>
> The third day is a straight run for Camp Anaconda. This is dangerous work for our drivers,

Sand, Grit and Dangerous Supply Missions

with explosive devices, or IEDs, or a constant threat of rocket-propelled grenades, land mines, mortars, and small-arms fire and spikes in the road. On a recent trip a 25-truck convoy suffered serious damage to 17 windshields from rocks thrown in two particular hostile cities. That is not unusual.

Sadly, 14 drivers have been killed while carrying out this important mission. That's 14 drivers. One driver, Al Caton, was also a friend of mine, as you heard in previous testimony. Al was a real leader and one of the nicest guys I know. Some of the other drivers were killed in the coordinated ambushes of convoys on April 8th and 9th, and two drivers are still missing from those tragic days. These drivers are a brave and courageous group of people.

But the danger does not end when the driving does. Even simply being at Camp Anaconda can be dangerous. In my 6 weeks in Anaconda this spring, there was virtually mortar fire every night, which means you get up, wait, go to the bunker and pray. At Anaconda I was asleep in my containerized housing when a mortar came flying just over my sleeping area and slammed into a KBR mail van parked 15 feet away.

Earlier this month at the same camp, a number of KBR employees had gathered for a July 4th celebration when two mortars hit. Twelve employees were injured, and three had to be evacuated to a combat support hospital. These close brushes with danger are not unusual for the men and women of KBR working in Iraq. It is simply a part of the job.

I also want to address some of the allegations made today. First was that we abandoned trucks

Chapter 12 The Fallout and Wounds You Can't See

because of flat tires or simple repairs. The Army provides all security, tells us what to deliver, when to travel and what routes to take. Contrary to some assertions, if a truck breaks down or is disabled, the decision to abandon or destroy a truck is made by the Army, not KBR. The Army makes a judgment based on their assessment of how best to save lives, not just equipment or trucks. KBR is the only contractor in Iraq with satellite tracking of its assets and personnel, and full recovery capability. Even a seemingly simple matter like changing a tire is at least a half-hour project.

So the Army must make difficult decisions. Let me repeat this. The Army, not KBR, makes all decisions regarding whether to halt the convoy, fix a truck or abandon it. We are operating in a war zone. The Army also provides records for driving, including security issues. We are told to run tight convoys and not allow intervening civilian vehicles, but the Army does not direct KBR to run civilians off the road. KBR, in fact, has disciplined several drivers who were found to have caused an accident by doing so. Several were terminated.

It has been said that we do not maintain our vehicles. That's not true. Today our teams of mechanics conduct routine preventive maintenance of each truck every 2 weeks. Current readiness rate is 81 percent and has never fallen below 75 percent.

While theft is not rampant, it is a problem. Protection of supplies from theft, it is the responsibility of the Army, and when thefts do occur, KBR promptly reports incidents to the Army. Cargo is

```
tracked by radio frequency system making paperwork
unnecessary.

    Mr. Chairman, we are doing everything humanly
possible to support our troops. I know you would
be proud of us if you saw us in action.

    Thank you for the opportunity to address you,
and I look forward to your questions.
```

I was first questioned by Republican Representative Ed Schrock of Virginia's 2nd District. His questions were straightforward and effectively countered the claims made by the whistleblowers. I explained that the two drivers had been terminated for conduct issues, including running Iraqi civilians off the road.

Next came Democratic Representative Brenda Watson from New Jersey, who tried to substantiate the whistleblowers' claims—but those assertions didn't hold up under scrutiny either.

After the testimony concluded, we were escorted to an off-site location to debrief with KBR's executive staff. When we entered the room, the team applauded and congratulated us. Another surreal moment in the strange, high-stakes world of LOGCAP, circa 2004.

By then, Lana and the boys had returned to Texas. That evening, I had dinner with the KBR staff and the consulting team. The next morning, I boarded a plane and headed back to Kuwait to finish what I had started.

Just another chapter in a year that had changed me forever.

CHAPTER 13
RETURN HOME AND LITIGATION

Over my final months in theater, I became fully immersed in the contractor lifestyle. I had lost all sense of reality of ever going home or being truly present with my real family and friends. Kuwait and the contracting staff had become my world. I had genuinely lost touch with what was real.

Now deeply connected to the contractor lifestyle, I was recruited by a former KBR executive—then working with a Kuwaiti Royal Family that owned the national postal service. The offer was to lead Kuwait's entire postal operation and join their board, with plans to relocate Lana and the boys and assist with purchasing a home. In my mindset at the time, it seemed like a real opportunity, and I tried to convince Lana. But she was emotionally exhausted and wanted no part of it. She just wanted me home and for us to return to a normal life. I was confused and frustrated, but in the end, I declined the offer.

I agreed to one final trip to Anaconda to meet with representatives of KBR's press corps and members of the media working on another short documentary about TTM. I saw it as my farewell tour. While there, I said my goodbyes to the staff and had the chance to visit with Art, thanking him for his dedication, loyalty, and leadership.

During my final weeks in Kuwait, B.G. Stultz was also completing his tour after nearly two years in theater, and he invited me—along with one other civilian—to his going-away gathering. His bio is impressive. He had deployed to Kuwait in October 2002 as commander of the 143rd Transportation Command, establishing initial logistics operations in support of Operation Iraqi Freedom. Advancing into Iraq with the initial ground offensive, he set up the first forward logistics hub at Tallil and launched initial rail operations at Garma, west of Baghdad. By October 2003, he had been assigned as Director of Movements, Distribution, and Transportation for the Coalition Forces Land Component Command-Kuwait, where he was responsible for the deployment and redeployment of sustainment supplies for U.S. and Coalition forces. From January to August 2004, he managed port and ground transportation operations for what became the largest movement of forces since World War II commonly referred to as "the surge." He returned to the U.S. in August 2004 after 22 months in theater.

In October 2004, Stultz was promoted to major general and assumed command of the 143rd Transportation Command in Orlando, Florida, overseeing twelve units in the southeastern United States. I was honored to be invited and, of course, I accepted. During his speech, he made a point to mention me. While speaking about civilian support to the military, he said, "And then there's Keith Richard—a civilian logistics professional leading a military operation in Iraq. The worst part is he had to put up with us generals." Everyone laughed, and I was touched to be included in such a meaningful moment even if I didn't quite agree with the characterization of "leading a military operation."

The KBR leadership staff also surprised me with a farewell event of their own. Around 100 people attended, including several key staff members—and, most meaningfully to me, a number of

Chapter 13 Return Home and Litigation

truck drivers. It was an emotional gathering. During my speech, I shared memories from my time overseas—some difficult, some rewarding.

On my last day in Kuwait, I stepped out of my office and left my boots outside the door. I said as many goodbyes as I could manage without losing my composure. British Ray drove me to the airport. We exchanged goodbyes, and I thanked him for his support.

As I flew home, my emotions shifted into a strange mix of confusion and emptiness. What am I going to do now? Who am I? How do I transition back into the business world and normal life in the U.S.? Along with that confusion came a growing sense of regret.

When I walked out of the terminal, Lana was waiting for me. We hugged and kissed, but she could immediately tell that I was distant. She understood that there would be a transition period and gave me space. We walked out to the parking lot and got into the Titan. She said she had a surprise for me. As we drove, I stayed silent and withdrawn. When we passed our home in McKinney, I asked where she was going. She told me she'd booked a cabin in Broken Bow, Oklahoma, for a few days so we could reconnect. I appreciated her thoughtfulness, but in my state of mind, I needed more than a cabin and a few quiet days.

Over those next few days, we tried to reconnect, but I wasn't ready. In my mind, I was still overseas, unable to break free from the past twelve months. I returned home exactly one year to the day from when I had first deployed. I remained on KBR's payroll through the end of November and still carried my Kuwait mobile phone with a 281-area code. While at the cabin, I used that phone to call British Ray, Art, and other staff members. Lana knew this would take time, and she was patient. But this was only the beginning.

When we returned home, I spent my days sitting in a recliner, reading emails from the KBR staff and staying updated on TTM. I still had my KBR-issued laptop. In December, I started a new role with a local intermodal trucking company that had recruited me while I was still overseas. The owner was familiar with my work and had spoken to me during my time in Kuwait. He'd launched the company with a seasoned trucking veteran, and I was brought in as VP of Operations.

But I wasn't ready for "normal." I was still angry, lost, and trying to find my footing. The operation itself was chaotic, disorganized, and lacked basic business structure. I frequently lashed out at drivers and staff and had numerous conversations with the owner about the systemic issues. It wasn't a healthy situation. Still, because of my industry relationships, we landed two large container shipping clients over the next few months—tripling the company's revenue. It felt like déjà vu: fast growth and chaos, just without the bombs and bullets.

Fortunately, I stayed in touch with a friend from Ryder, Dave, whom I'd worked with during my first one-year stint there from 2000 to 2001. We'd developed mutual respect, and while I was overseas, he stayed in regular contact. In March 2005, Ryder offered me a manager position overseeing the Cadbury Adams account. It wasn't a senior leadership role, but it gave me the chance to decompress—and gave Lana and me space to focus on our next chapter.

Meanwhile, sometime during December 2004, I drove to Houston to return my laptop. During that time the person I was having an affair with inside Kuwait was on R&R in Houston and we agreed to have dinner. Confused, regretful and still attempting to understand a new reality, I accepted. My armor was slowly coming down at home and it was becoming more and more apparent that all the insanity had to stop. We had dinner and said goodbye and agreed that this wasn't something we could continue.

Chapter 13 Return Home and Litigation

When I returned home, I continued texting with the staff in Kuwait on their 281-area code phones. I also sent a message to *her*, saying it was good to see her in Houston and wishing her the best. Something inside me said it was time to break the insanity. It was killing me, and it couldn't go on.

I purposely left my phone on the kitchen counter, thinking, *Lana will read the text, and whatever comes next is for the best.* Sure enough, she saw the message. Her face flooded with anger and heartbreak. I knew immediately. And while I didn't know what came next, I knew one thing for certain: Lana didn't deserve this. It was time to figure this out. But I had no idea how. I was a lost soul, full of regret and rage.

She left the house and called two close friends—both fellow Christians with whom we shared a strong bond of faith. One of them told her, "You're not going to leave. You're going to fight for your relationship." To this day, I still thank her. That was the turning point—the start of what would become a long road to reconciliation.

Between our faith in the Lord Jesus Christ, support from friends and family, marriage counseling, therapy (which ultimately led to a PTSD diagnosis), and a book called *Torn Asunder*, we slowly found our way back. Ryder also gave me the flexibility I needed. That season of our lives was painfully difficult, but it may offer hope to other couples on the journey of forgiveness, commitment, and faith. True love can be rediscovered. Life *can* continue.

Litigation

In 2005, four families of drivers killed on April 8th and 9th filed a wrongful death suit against KBR and Halliburton in Texas. Two other families of injured drivers filed additional lawsuits. Fourteen KBR drivers were killed in Iraq in 2004: six at various times throughout the year, one on April 8th, and seven on the tragic day of April 9th.

Halliburton wasn't involved in the day-to-day operations and was only named because of its parent affiliation with KBR. (They sold KBR in 2007.)

The lawsuit alleged that KBR leadership knew the convoys were vulnerable on April 9th—the one-year anniversary of the fall of Baghdad—and that they had received numerous warnings of increased hostile activity. Despite this, the complaint claimed, KBR misled drivers about the risks during recruiting and orientation.

KBR cited the Defense Base Act as a basis for dismissal. The act provides legal protections to contractors under Department of Defense contracts. After years of litigation, testimony, and hearings, on January 12, 2012, the Fifth Circuit Court of Appeals in New Orleans dismissed the lawsuit, citing the Defense Base Act.

As mentioned earlier, Sharron Stagg, Assistant General Counsel for KBR, and I remained close acquaintances for over fifteen years. This was one of many lawsuits associated with LOGCAP III—some of which are still pending to this day. I was deposed three more times in connection with various contract issues, the most recent in 2020. Even though I had resigned from KBR in 2004, Sharron and I stayed in touch, and KBR provided legal representation for each deposition.

To me, the April 8th and 9th lawsuit felt like the final chapter of chaos and insanity. Sharron and I spoke late in 2004 and agreed that lawsuits tied to LOGCAP III would likely stretch on for decades, and that the April 9th incident would be just one of many.

T. Scott Allen Jr. served as the lead attorney for two of the deceased drivers, while others were represented by different attorneys. Mr. Allen led a seven-year effort to litigate the deaths, ultimately seeking $2 billion in damages from KBR and Halliburton.

Chapter 13 Return Home and Litigation

The case passed through District Courts and the U.S. House Oversight and Reform Committee.

Because of my position with KBR and involvement in the events of April 9th, I was one of several former employees deposed—and considered the lead witness in Allen's case. KBR delayed my deposition for as long as possible, hoping the case would be dismissed. I was at the top of Mr. Allen's "deposed" list. Eventually, the deposition was scheduled, and the echoes of Iraq's chaos returned full force.

It was set for December 4, 2008. At that point, Lana and I were working hard to rebuild our lives. The last thing either of us wanted was to be pulled back into that darkness. But I had no choice.

I was represented by Haynes and Boone, a top-100 law firm based in Dallas with 700 lawyers across nineteen offices. They had successfully represented Dick Cheney in the 2000 election litigation. One of the attorneys from that case was now overseeing mine. My lead attorney, Michael Warnecke, worked alongside a team of KBR lawyers who also provided support.

The deaths of April 8th and 9th still haunt me. As one of the drivers, Randy Ross, once said, "Neither KBR nor the military are at fault." He blamed Iraq. "It was a bad day. A very bad day."

Ultimately, the Army had the responsibility to assess threat levels and provide force protection. As previously noted, all hell broke loose that day. The military's decisions, threat assessments, and communications were second-guessed and scrutinized in the aftermath.

The weeks leading up to the deposition were brutal. I was forced to relive those tragic events—decisions, conversations, thousands of emails. As I've said throughout this book, I was emotionally raw, angry, and deeply frustrated—and all of it came through in my emails. Mr. Allen used them as his primary source of evidence during my 20-hour deposition, which spanned three days from

December 4th through December 6, 2008. Almost exactly four years after my employment with KBR.

At the same time, I was juggling a demanding full-time position at Ryder. Thankfully, the company was incredibly supportive and allowed me the flexibility I needed. Even so, the process was mentally and emotionally draining, distracting me from my job and my family.

I met with attorneys from Haynes and Boone, KBR, and others—both via conference calls and in person. There were moments when I could barely think straight. I was confused, emotional, unsure if I could withstand what felt like a direct assault on my integrity and character. Mike, my attorney, would call for breaks to help me stay composed and focused on the facts.

The deposition was held at Haynes and Boone's offices in Dallas. Around fifteen to twenty people attended representing me, KBR, the plaintiffs, and several family members of the deceased drivers. I sat at the head of a long conference table. Mike was on my left; Mr. Allen was on my right. After I was sworn in, the verbal barrage began.

Mr. Allen had a five-inch stack of emails fully highlighted, annotated, weaponized. He went straight into questioning my emails and decisions. At one point, gesturing to the families in the room, he said, "Mr. Richard, you killed the husbands and fathers of these families." Mike immediately objected. I wanted to reach across the table and knock the guy out. It was clear his goal was to break me.

I asked for a break to regain my composure. Day one was rough, but I managed to find some rhythm by days two and three. When the final minute ticked off the clock, I stood to leave. Mr. Allen announced that two minutes remained due to a procedural technicality. He insisted on continuing his questions about a conversation I had with Major Andrews and Lt. Col. Davidson on April 9. I told him I didn't recall the details, and if I did, the information

Chapter 13 Return Home and Litigation

was classified. He refused to accept my response and pressed on. A KBR attorney argued that I had already answered and reiterated the classified nature of the discussion.

At my attorney Mike's request, we went off the record. Mike then asked me to give Mr. Allen the remaining two minutes. Frustrated, I agreed. We went back on record, and Mr. Allen kept pressing. I stuck to my answer: "I don't recall, and if I did, it was classified." All I wanted at that point was to get the hell out of there and never look back.

After some twenty hours—sixteen of them on the record and videotaped—what were two more minutes? I sat down. Mr. Allen spent those final moments trying to get me to recall a classified conversation between me and two military officers in a secure room. I told him what I'd told him before: I didn't remember. And I didn't.

When it was finally over, I stood up, shook hands with everyone, except Mr. Allen, and left the building. I didn't say a word. I didn't want to. As far as I was concerned, this was the last chapter. I never wanted to look back.

CHAPTER 14

CONCLUSION

I was deposed on three other occasions over a 12-year span, all related to contract issues. I was also contacted by the FBI about the flatbed leasing incident involving the terminated transportation manager and assistant transportation manager. I'm not certain of the exact outcome or final disposition for those two individuals. I kept in touch with Sharron about all the various legal matters, and KBR continued to provide legal support.

I forgot to mention that I was in Kuwait when Saddam Hussein was captured. For those who may not know, he was the President of Iraq and considered target number one by the U.S. military. He was found hiding in a hole and didn't resist arrest. While that was a significant moment for the military, it was barely a blip on the radar for KBR and TTM.

Now, here we are—20 years later. After many conversations and some gentle persuasion from my two sons, Keith Jr. and Aaron, and my good friend Bill, I decided it was finally time to tell my story—and the story of the brave civilians who supported our troops. Lana and I only spoke about the book a few times. It wasn't something she wanted to relive. We've moved forward into a beautiful life together—now 43 years strong and counting. We're surrounded by amazing friends and family and have a second home in Ocean Springs, Mississippi, which has brought us back to our roots.

We travel to the Mississippi Gulf Coast often to spend time with family and reconnect with both old and new acquaintances. And most importantly—fresh seafood. We buy shrimp straight off the boats for $2 to $3 a pound. I also love to fish, and the "Gulf of America" delivers some incredible fishing. There's nothing like it.

But most of all—especially for Lana—our greatest joy is our five grandchildren. They all live in North Texas and are a big part of our lives. Lillian (17) and Emilia (16) are Keith Jr.'s daughters, while Oliver (9), Finley (5), and Theodore "Teddy" (18 months) are Aaron and Mary's boys. We babysit Teddy twice a week and even attempted to watch all five for three days in November 2024. As my mom used to say, "There's a reason the Lord gave children to young people."

Life has brought Lana and me many trials and tribulations, but it's been an incredible journey—one built on patience, commitment, love, and our faith in the Lord Jesus Christ. Looking back, there are things I might've done differently—decisions I regret. But I couldn't ask for more than what we've overcome and achieved together.

I wouldn't be where I am today without Lana's love, guidance, and support. She's a tough cookie and has stood by my side through every high and low. She's helped shape me into a better man, and a better husband. She even taught me the fine art of loading a dishwasher, folding clothes, straightening the couch cushions, and ensuring the toilet paper rolls over the top. As I said at the beginning, there's "a" way—and then there's Lana's way. I'm all in on Lana's way.

I can't change what happened in 2004. The past is part of my journey. Over the years, I've shared pieces of these experiences

Chapter 14 Conclusion

with colleagues, friends, and family, though not everything. Some of what is captured in these pages may be unexpected, and I share it now with humility and the hope that it's received with understanding and grace.

People often ask, "Why did you take the job in Iraq?" Honestly, I'm still not entirely sure. I've always had deep respect for the military. My father-in-law was a veteran of WWII, Korea, and Vietnam. I spoke with him about the opportunity, and, of course, he was supportive. Those earlier conflicts defined their generations. Iraq, it seemed, would define mine. I guess I saw it as an opportunity to serve our great country—and yes, as a career move. It was another angle on logistics.

The bigger question is: why did I—and so many other contractors—*stay* in Iraq? That part's easier to answer. Loyalty. Commitment. Patriotism. Team. These are deeply held American values. Sure, the compensation was generous, but no one stayed in a life-or-death situation just for the money.

Throughout my life, I've held leadership roles in complex organizations. I've always been committed to supporting a team. As I mentioned in Chapter One, that commitment sometimes manifests as passionate defense of team members, and at times, frustration that leads to conflict with internal organizations that support or lack in supporting my teams. Anyone who's worked with me over the years would likely agree.

So, who are the true heroes of the Iraq War? Certainly, the military. There are countless stories of individual bravery and sacrifice. And while it may have been a "smaller" war than WWII, Korea, or Vietnam, the frontline was everywhere. The casualty lists and the trauma speak for themselves.

But there were other heroes too—unsung ones. The brave civilians who supported the military under hostile, chaotic, and dangerous conditions. During my tenure, 14 TTM drivers were killed, and over 700 trucks and trailers were damaged or destroyed.

We were in a war—whether we expected to be or not. I may be biased, but I knew these men and women. Many of them put their lives on the line every day to ensure our troops had what they needed to fight. Some never came home. They were heroes, too. This book is my story—and theirs.

Finally, I didn't watch the Presidential Medal of Freedom ceremony in 2024. The criteria for recipients are clear: significant contributions to (1) the security or national interest of the U.S., (2) world peace, or (3) cultural or public endeavors. Frankly, I didn't feel all the recipients met those standards. But as I watched clips afterward, my thoughts turned to the unsung heroes of Iraq. The civilians. The drivers. The team. They deserve that kind of recognition. Maybe one day, they'll get it.